FOURTH GRADE SURVIVAL GUIDE

Fun Tips, Exam Strategies, & Puzzles To Rock
4th Grade Like a Superstar!

Bobbie Anderson Jr

Copyright 2025 by Bobbie Anderson Jr.
- ALL Rights Reserved

In no way is it legal to reproduce, duplicate, or transmit any part of this document in either electronic means or in printed format. Recording of this publication is strictly prohibited and any storage of this document is not allowed unless with written permission from the publisher.

Thank you for buying our book and supporting our mission to provide accessible resources for everyone!

Instructions for Word Search Puzzles

- Hidden words are key vocabulary of each chapter
- Some words are combined. For example, "fourth grade" is hidden as "fourthgrade".
- Words are hidden in forward, horizontal, vertical, in reverse, and four diagonal directions (top-left, top-right, bottom-left, bottom-right).
- STUCK? The parenthesis shows combined words.

To avoid any potential bleed-through while solving word search puzzles with certain pens or markers, simply place a blank sheet of thicker paper behind the page you're working on.

This guide is more than just a book—it's a comprehensive fourth grade study resource designed to address every aspect of a student's journey. Whether your child is mastering math, navigating group projects, or preparing for exams, the Fourth Grade Survival Guide will help your child rock fourth grade like a SUPERSTAR!

Each chapter ends with a fun word search puzzle that reinforces key concepts, making learning enjoyable and helping kids retain knowledge effectively.

LET'S GO!

Table of Contents

Chapter 1: How to Own Your First Day of Fourth Grade 7

Chapter 2: How to Pick the Right Friends in Fourth Grade 15

Chapter 3: How to Handle Disagreements in the Fourth-Grade Classroom 23

Chapter 4: How to Handle Disagreements on the Playground in Fourth Grade 31

Chapter 5: How to Ask the Right Questions in Fourth Grade 39

Chapter 6: How to Work Together in Small Groups in Fourth Grade 47

Chapter 7: How to Crush Fourth Grade History 55

Chapter 8: How to Succeed in Fourth Grade Math 63

Chapter 9: How to Read Like a Pro in Fourth Grade 71

Chapter 10: How to Succeed in Fourth Grade P.E. 79

Chapter 11: How to Rock Fourth Grade Science 87

Chapter 12: How to Write Like a Pro in Fourth Grade 95

Chapter 13: How to Conquer Fourth Grade Homework Like a Pro 103

Chapter 14: How to Ace Fourth Grade Exams 111

Word Search Solutions .... 119 - 134

BELONGS TO

....

Chapter 1

How to Own Your First Day of Fourth Grade

Hey, fourth grader-to-be! Starting a new school year is a big deal, and moving up to fourth grade? That's huge. You've got more independence, bigger challenges, and a fresh chance to make this your best year yet. The first day might feel exciting, scary, or both—but don't worry. This chapter has tons of tips and real-life ideas to help you rock that first day like a pro. Let's go!

1. Dress for Success (and Confidence!)
Pick out clothes that make you feel comfortable and confident. Fourth grade is about expressing yourself, so wear something that shows your style, whether it's a favorite T-shirt or cool sneakers.

Real-Life Scenario:
You wear your lucky blue hoodie on the first day because it makes you feel unstoppable. When your new teacher says, "Nice hoodie!" you're already off to a great start.

2. Be Prepared Like A Pro
Check your school supply list and pack your backpack the night before. Having everything you need—like pencils, notebooks, and maybe a cool new binder—helps you feel ready for anything.

Real-Life Scenario:
Your teacher asks everyone to pull out their highlighters. You're one of the first to have yours ready, and your classmates are impressed. Way to start off prepared!

3. Smile and Say Hello
It's normal to feel a little nervous meeting new classmates or seeing old ones after the summer. Start by smiling and saying "Hi" to someone—it's an easy way to break the ice.

Real-Life Scenario:
You sit next to a kid you don't know during morning meeting. You say, "Hi, I'm Jordan. What's your favorite subject?" They smile back and say, "Science!" Boom—you just made your first fourth-grade friend.

4. Pay Attention to Your Teacher's Rules
Fourth grade usually means more responsibility, so listen closely when your teacher talks about classroom rules and expectations. Write them down if it helps you remember.

Real-Life Scenario:
Your teacher explains the new system for earning "classroom bucks." You write it down so you can start planning how to save up for a cool reward, like extra recess.

5. Get to Know Your Schedule
Fourth grade might have a more complicated schedule than last year. You might switch classrooms for different subjects or have a new specials rotation. Pay attention to where you're supposed to go and when.

Real-Life Scenario:
You almost go to art when it's actually gym, but you remember checking the schedule that morning. Crisis averted—you show up in sneakers and are ready for action.

6. Stay Organized

This year, you'll probably have more assignments and responsibilities. Use folders, notebooks, or even an agenda to keep track of homework and important papers. Starting organized on Day 1 helps you stay on top of things.

Real-Life Scenario:
Your teacher gives you a math worksheet and a reading log to take home. Instead of crumpling them into your backpack, you neatly place them in your homework folder. You're already feeling like a fourth-grade pro.

7. Speak Up and Ask Questions

If you're not sure about something, don't be afraid to ask. Fourth-grade teachers love when students are curious and want to understand more.

Real-Life Scenario:
Your teacher explains a new rule about recess equipment, but you're confused. You raise your hand and ask, "Can we still use the soccer balls?" Your teacher says yes, and now everyone knows—thanks to you!

8. Try Sitting with Someone New

Even if you're excited to see your old friends, the first day is a perfect chance to make new ones. Sit with someone you don't know at lunch or during group activities.

Real-Life Scenario:
You sit next to a new student at lunch and ask about their summer. They tell you about their trip to the Grand Canyon, and you bond over how cool it sounds. By the end of lunch, you've made a new buddy.

9. Be Ready for New Challenges
Fourth grade might mean harder math problems, longer writing assignments, or more in-depth science projects. Instead of worrying, think of it as a chance to level up your skills.

Real-Life Scenario:
Your teacher hands out a multiplication review sheet, and some of the problems look tricky. Instead of panicking, you think, "I'll give it my best shot!" When you finish, you feel super proud of yourself.

10. Show Off Your Fourth-Grade Confidence
Fourth graders are role models for younger students, so walk in with your head held high. Act kind, responsible, and ready to help.

Real-Life Scenario:
A second grader in the hallway drops their pencil case. You pick it up for them and say, "Here you go!" They look up at you like you're a superhero. Fourth-grade win!

11. Don't Sweat the Small Stuff
If something doesn't go perfectly—like you forget your lunchbox or trip in the hallway—don't worry! Mistakes happen, and they're part of learning.

Real-Life Scenario:
You accidentally call your teacher "Mom." Everyone giggles, but instead of getting embarrassed, you laugh too. The moment passes, and your day keeps going great.

12. End the Day Strong
Before you head home, make sure you have everything you need: homework, notes for your parents, and any supplies. Take a moment to think about something awesome that happened that day.

Real-Life Scenario:
You grab your reading log and remember how you helped someone in class figure out a tricky word. As you walk out, you feel proud and ready to take on the rest of the year.

Final Thought
The first day of fourth grade is your chance to set the tone for an amazing year. By being prepared, staying confident, and making the most of every moment, you'll show everyone, including yourself—that you're ready to shine. You've got this, fourth grader! Now go out there and make it an awesome first day!

Chapter 1 How to Own Your First Day of Fourth Grade

```
S E L H E E A L U M Y L S D C C S T F K W P O
M C H A L L E N G E S R J Z G S E T X R Q R M
Q L Y J R I J F E Q G Z V D G C L P B X P D A
A S E C I M M P E J O F X W V V U R P D S J M
B N C J D S U O O E P Y H T Y Q R D I O Q E N
N K E H K Y A X U P H Y Y O M Y V Z F Z E Z J
X V X V E E T A Y G X T C R T D Z P M G Z L B
J G C A S D C S A A L C U Y M S U F H O H I C
X Y R Z I N U H A F M Y P C Z W O R M E B A F
Y T Q P V K O L C Y E Z F Q S U P E R H E R O
D B W Z W W Z I E W L R I I R H Y O D Q A Y W
H Q I A N X H E T U Q I A T R Q E Y V O E U S
Y D S A F C O S K S O F H P K S P B R P H N Y
K K W Z T B L N S C E G Q Y E V T G A Y X K A
E Z K H N T Q U O G R U Q B S R A D Z R O C U
H L Y Y Z C G N M A G U Q M C N P R A Y X K L
P S O X O M F D D C Y H N P I S F G M Y O P S
J R U R Y I X E C A F V J Z K B Z S D V G U O
Q Y P B D G P U O M O B E S O L R M P Y C L K
T M S E G J I Y N E W P D Q K J V E Y C K X H
T V N I J R K K N D P U K A E P S B E H W B Q
F C K T Z T N B L E R J V E N Q M S R Z S A Z
E J J J G W L X H L R X H Z Q H S S I Z P P W
```

ask
challenges
confidence
firstday (first day)
fourthgrade
(fourth grade)
organize
prepare
questions
role
rules
schedule
smile
speakup (speak up)
success
superhero

Chapter 2

How to Pick the Right Friends in Fourth Grade

Hey there, friendship expert! Fourth grade is an awesome time to make new friends and strengthen old ones. But let's be real—not everyone you meet will be a perfect fit for you. The good news is that you can choose friends who make you laugh, support you, and help you be the best version of yourself. In this chapter, we'll explore tons of ideas and real-life scenarios to help you find and pick the right friends for fourth grade. Let's jump in!

1. Look for Shared Interests
Best friendships often start with something in common. Whether it's a love for video games, sports, or drawing, shared interests are a great foundation for a fun friendship.

Real-Life Scenario:
You love basketball and notice a kid at recess practicing free throws. You join them and say, "Want to play one-on-one?" By the end of recess, you've not only had a blast but also found someone who loves the game as much as you do.

2. Pay Attention to Kindness
Good friends are kind—not just to you, but to everyone around them. Watch how people treat others, like classmates, teachers, or even the quiet kid at the back of the room.

Real-Life Scenario:
You see a classmate helping another student pick up their dropped supplies without being asked. You think, "Wow, they're really nice!" Later, you ask if they want to sit with you at lunch, and you start building a great friendship.

3. Choose Friends Who Support You

The right friends cheer you on when you do something awesome and help you when you're feeling down. Avoid people who try to put you down or make fun of your ideas.

Real-Life Scenario:

You share your dream of becoming an astronaut during a class project. One classmate says, "That's so cool!" while another rolls their eyes and says, "You'll never do that." Who would you rather hang out with? The cheerleader, of course!

4. Be Open to New People

Your best friend doesn't have to be just like you. Sometimes, the most amazing friendships happen when you get to know someone different.

Real-Life Scenario:

You usually sit with the same group during lunch, but one day, you join a quiet kid who's reading a book about dragons. You strike up a conversation and discover you both love fantasy stories. Friendship unlocked!

5. Watch Out for Negative Behavior

Not everyone you meet will treat you or others well. If someone is bossy, rude, or always wants things their way, it's okay to step back and focus on finding kinder friends.

Real-Life Scenario:

A kid at recess always demands to be the team captain and yells if they don't win. You decide to join a different group that laughs and has fun no matter what. Smart move!

6. Stand Up for Yourself
Good friends respect your boundaries. If someone teases you or makes you feel uncomfortable, speak up. True friends will listen and try to make things right.

Real-Life Scenario:
Your friend keeps calling you a nickname you don't like. You say, "Hey, I don't really like that name. Can you stop?" If they apologize and stop, they're showing respect. If not, it might be time to find a new friend.

7. Find Friends Who Make You Laugh
Laughter is one of the best parts of friendship! Look for people who share your sense of humor and enjoy being silly with you.

Real-Life Scenario:
During a group project, someone cracks a joke about a funny mistake, and you can't stop laughing. By the end of the project, you've both created an inside joke that makes working together even more fun.

8. Balance Your Time
It's okay to have more than one friend. In fact, having a mix of friends can make your school year even better. Try to spend time with different people instead of sticking to just one person all the time.

Real-Life Scenario:
You spend recess playing soccer with one group of friends but sit with a different group at lunch to talk about your favorite books. Both groups make you happy, so you enjoy the best of both worlds.

9. Watch for Red Flags

Sometimes, friends might act in ways that aren't okay. If someone is mean, tries to make you do things you're uncomfortable with, or leaves you out on purpose, it's important to recognize that behavior.

Real-Life Scenario:
A friend says, "If you don't let me copy your homework, I won't be your friend anymore." That's a red flag. True friends wouldn't pressure you like that. It's okay to say no and focus on healthier friendships.

10. Be a Good Friend Yourself

Friendship is a two-way street. If you want great friends, be a great friend! Show kindness, be trustworthy, and cheer on your pals.

Real-Life Scenario:
Your friend is nervous about a class presentation. You say, "You've got this—I know you'll do awesome!" Later, they thank you for your encouragement, and your bond grows even stronger.

11. Give New Friendships Time

Not every friendship happens instantly. Sometimes, it takes time to get to know someone and build trust.

Real-Life Scenario:
A new student joins your class, and you start by saying "Hi" and asking how they like the school. Over the next few weeks, you talk more and discover you both love animals. Now, you're great friends.

12. Trust Your Gut

If someone makes you feel happy and supported, they're probably a good friend. If someone makes you feel uncomfortable or upset, trust your instincts and take a step back.

Real-Life Scenario:

You hang out with a group at recess, but they keep excluding others and gossiping. It doesn't feel right, so you decide to join a different group that's more welcoming. Good call!

Final Thought

Fourth grade is an exciting time to meet new people and build awesome friendships. By choosing kind, supportive friends and being a great friend yourself, you'll create connections that make this year unforgettable. Remember, the right friends make you feel happy, valued, and confident. So go out there and find your crew—you've got this!

Chapter 2 How to Pick the Right Friends in Fourth Grade

```
Q S M X A P M E F G B O R Y M U L L N K B Z F
Y J N V P L S I Z D F N P X H J C Y D F G X U
Q L L O F P Q R D L M C P W E Q J S B V C A O
K D K B I N N R E H N I O R W H C F Z A I E U
P N T D E T C I V I B S N M K Y J Q L T H N L
Y H P N I H C X S O T K Y N M B W W W G P Y H
D J H A N I A E U Y K O H X H O K H G J K X G
D I T U T S H V N S U N B T Y E N M T T P O C
X S S V E X B Z I N U R Q Z D L X L D Q L Q T
A T E Z R O G M T O O Q P L F K X P X A F Y P
T P L B E O N G M H R C F K Q N M K Y C L O Y
O H R F S C H V W D W Z G N P R F G U G E J T
M M G U T E E R Q O B K D Z W R N R L Z X L D
T T V I O M K R T V B H O R P D H T I Q I N T
E R R S R K X H O K W F C S S F C G R E Q G F
O P D O T G B X Z A J T G V G R P K Y U N E O
O F C C P A V D R Q T H B A L A N C E S J D W
O S K W K P N E T C T E K E T W L V W O F E S
B S E G C E U D X W W B P C B F E F M N N Y G
G M P T I M E S U A S S E N D N I K D C B F R
M F Q Y R Z Y Y J P M E K J Q C J Q I E N Y A
U H G U A L A P J M C Z X J X A A P K D R X L
Q T R U S T W O R T H Y K K D V U E B L E Y I
```

balance   interest   right
behavior   kindness   standup
common   laugh   support
connections   new   time
friends   redflags (red flags)   trustworthy

Chapter 3

How to Handle Disagreements in the Fourth-Grade Classroom

Hey, future peacemaker! Fourth grade is a big year where you'll work with classmates, share ideas, and tackle cool projects. But sometimes, disagreements can pop up—and that's totally normal. The good news is, with a few smart strategies, you can handle conflicts like a pro. In this chapter, we'll explore how to solve problems, keep things cool, and even turn disagreements into chances to learn and grow. Let's dive in!

1. Take a Step Back
When you feel frustrated, it's easy to say something you might regret. Instead, take a moment to pause. Stepping back gives you time to calm down and think clearly.

Real-Life Scenario:
You and your classmate both want to be the leader for a group project. You feel your face getting hot, so you take a deep breath and say, "Let's talk about this after we both cool off for a minute." Later, you come back ready to work things out.

2. Use "I" Statements
When you're in a disagreement, blaming the other person can make things worse. Instead, talk about how you feel by using "I" statements. This helps keep the conversation respectful.

Real-Life Scenario:
A friend takes your pencil without asking, and instead of saying, "You're always taking my stuff!" you say, "I feel upset when you take my pencil without asking. Can you please ask next time?" Now you're solving the problem instead of starting an argument.

3. Be Open to Different Opinions

In fourth grade, you'll notice that not everyone thinks the same way—and that's okay! Being open to different ideas can turn a disagreement into a chance to learn something new.

Real-Life Scenario:
You're voting on a book for the class read-aloud, and your choice doesn't win. Instead of feeling upset, you think, "Maybe I'll like this book after all." Later, you realize it's one of the best stories you've ever read.

4. Work Together to Solve the Problem

Disagreements don't have to be about "winning" or "losing." Instead, try working together to find a solution that makes everyone happy.

Real-Life Scenario:
During recess, two classmates argue about whether to play soccer or tag. You step in and suggest, "What if we play soccer today and tag tomorrow?" Everyone agrees, and you all have fun.

5. Tone is Important

Your tone is how you say something. It is just as important as what you say. Even if you're frustrated, try to keep your voice calm and your words polite.

Real-Life Scenario:
A teammate in your group project isn't pulling their weight. Instead of yelling, you say calmly, "We need to finish this project together. Can you help with the next part?" Your calm tone helps them feel included instead of attacked.

6. Ask Questions to Understand
Sometimes, disagreements happen because people don't understand each other. Asking questions can help clear up confusion and bring you closer to solving the problem.

Real-Life Scenario:
Your partner in a science project wants to use a method you think won't work. Instead of arguing, you ask, "Why do you think that's the best way?" Their answer helps you see their perspective, and you come up with a new plan together.

7. Use Humor to Break the Tension
Laughter can help ease a disagreement and make everyone feel better—just make sure your joke isn't mean or aimed at someone else.

Real-Life Scenario:
You and a friend are arguing about who gets the last piece of colored paper for an art project. You hold it up and say, "Okay, let's arm-wrestle for it!" Everyone laughs, and you both decide to share the paper.

8. Know When to Get Help
Not all disagreements can be solved on your own. If the problem feels too big or someone is being unkind, it's okay to ask a teacher or adult for help.

Real-Life Scenario:
A classmate keeps interrupting you during group discussions, even after you've asked them to stop. You let your teacher know, and they help set up rules for taking turns to speak.

9. Practice Empathy

Empathy means trying to see things from someone else's point of view. When you understand how the other person feels, it's easier to find a solution.

Real-Life Scenario:
You get mad when your friend doesn't want to play your favorite game at recess. Later, you think about how they might feel—they've been playing your game all week and want a turn to choose. You apologize and agree to play their game tomorrow.

10. Learn to Let It Go

Not every disagreement needs a long conversation. Sometimes, it's better to let small things go and move on.

Real-Life Scenario:
Your friend calls you by a nickname you don't love, but you know they didn't mean to upset you. Instead of making a big deal, you laugh it off and let them know politely what you'd rather be called.

11. Celebrate Solutions

When you solve a disagreement, take a moment to feel proud. Handling conflicts well is a big step toward becoming more mature and confident.

Real-Life Scenario:
You and your classmate disagree about how to divide tasks in a group project. After talking it through, you split the work evenly. When you finish the project, you realize you worked together better than ever before.

12. Remember: Disagreements Are Normal

It's impossible to agree with everyone all the time, and that's okay. What matters is how you handle disagreements when they happen.

Real-Life Scenario:

You and your best friend have an argument about what to do after school. At first, you're both upset, but after a little time and a good conversation, you're back to laughing and hanging out. Disagreements didn't ruin your friendship—they made it stronger.

Final Thought

Disagreements happen, but they don't have to ruin your day. With kindness, patience, and a little creativity, you can handle any classroom conflict like a fourth-grade pro. Remember, every disagreement is a chance to practice teamwork, listening, and problem-solving. You've got this!

Chapter 3 How to Handle Disagreements in the Fourth-Grade Classroom

```
X X C L K Y X L N T H Z X K G M Q W H U W E H
M I L W Z H I C O U A C L A R O M P Y X G V Z
Y H T A P M E N E Y N L H I P O B G B B T Z K
J N P X A Q E R V C D U B I O C W X P W R D R
O P V Z F H S E O D L Z N R T B W J J Q B S M
B R O M U H R I M W E I S K N O F P D T L O Y
B N Y R C I Y J M I O S S O E P I B I V V Y N
R Q M S L E G U A N A R I O R G E B S J V P R
N E P Y O M L T S L G G R I E P F T A S K C E
L P J W T J W E C D G Y K J F O Z Q G B X M I
E G L U F Z N Q B N O W E A F Z E A R D T R S
F D W E U F I Z J R X W F V I S Z B E E J P T
L V V Z H M I B X Y A K N K D M L F E T P Z A
D G F P J J W K U Z C T L Y H L I N M A M J T
L U U D D Q B U E B N X E Y C K F Y E R P O E
F L V R A O G D Y I O U E Q K I T O N T M T M
B M V L N Q G R Y S K Z L K R E V H T S V V E
A N S D J O F M I X V L Q H M Y Y Q S U A F N
G U T G Q Y Z P P L A P P D T D R E O R L P T
L A J X V Z T M S P G Z G G C S T E V F E Y S
S U Y R G P A X B H Q N X M A J J R S M L M W
W S V V F D H L V W Q D B W I Z M L W Z B J W
R Z J A X Z L R E H T E G O T K C E M R C D D
```

celebrate   frustrated   moveon (move on)
classroom   handle   opinions
different   help   together
disagreements   humor   tone
empathy   istatements   work
                      (I statements)

Chapter 4

How to Handle Disagreements on the Playground in Fourth Grade

Hey, fourth-grade peacemaker! The playground is one of the best parts of the day—a place to run, play, and have fun with friends. But let's be real: sometimes, disagreements pop up. Maybe it's about whose turn it is, what game to play, or who gets the soccer ball first. Don't worry! Disagreements are normal, and this chapter will show you how to handle them like a playground pro. Let's get started!

1. Take a Deep Breath Before Reacting
When something doesn't go your way, it's easy to get upset. But before saying or doing something you might regret, take a deep breath. This gives you a chance to calm down and think clearly.

Real-Life Scenario:
You're waiting for the swing, but someone cuts in front of you. Instead of yelling, you take a deep breath and say, "Hey, I've been waiting. Can I have my turn now?" Staying calm helps keep things peaceful.

2. Speak Up for Yourself (But Stay Polite)
If something feels unfair, don't just stay quiet. Speak up—but use kind and respectful words. Being polite shows that you're serious without being mean.

Real-Life Scenario:
You're playing four square, and someone keeps changing the rules to benefit themselves. You say, "Hey, I think we should stick to the rules we started with. That way it's fair for everyone." Now you've addressed the problem without causing a fight.

3. Find a Compromise
Compromising means finding a solution that works for everyone. It's not about winning or losing—it's about working together.

Real-Life Scenario:
You and your friends can't decide whether to play soccer or tag. You suggest, "How about we play soccer first, then tag after?" Everyone agrees, and now you're all having fun.

4. Take Turns
A lot of playground disagreements come down to waiting for a turn. Sharing and taking turns show fairness and respect for others.

Real-Life Scenario:
There's only one basketball, and everyone wants to shoot hoops. You say, "Let's take turns shooting five shots each, then pass it to the next person." Problem solved, and now everyone gets to play.

5. Listen to Other Perspectives
Sometimes, a disagreement happens because people see things differently. Listening to the other person's side can help you understand where they're coming from.

Real-Life Scenario:
You think your team scored a goal in soccer, but the other team says the ball was out of bounds. Instead of arguing, you ask, "Why do you think it was out?" They explain their point of view, and you all agree to a do-over.

6. Use Rock, Paper, Scissors
For small disagreements, like who gets to go first or which game to play, let rock, paper, scissors decide. It's quick, fair, and takes the pressure off.

Real-Life Scenario:
You and your friend both want to be "it" for freeze tag. You play rock, paper, scissors, and they win. No hard feelings, you'll get the next turn.

7. Don't Take It Personally
Sometimes, people get frustrated or say things they don't mean during a disagreement. Try not to take it personally and focus on solving the problem instead.

Real-Life Scenario:
A friend snaps at you during a basketball game and says, "You're playing terrible defense!" Instead of getting upset, you respond, "I'll do better next round." Later, they apologize for being rude, and you move on.

8. Walk Away If You Need To
If a disagreement gets too heated, it's okay to take a break. Walking away gives everyone time to cool off and think about what really matters.

Real-Life Scenario:
You're arguing with someone about whether they cheated in four square. Instead of yelling, you say, "Let's take a break and come back to this later." After recess, you both feel calmer and can talk it out.

9. Get Creative with Solutions
Sometimes, thinking outside the box can solve playground disagreements in a fun way.

Real-Life Scenario:
Your group wants to play kickball, but another group is already on the field. You suggest, "What if we play kickball in the open space by the trees?" Everyone agrees, and now both groups are happy.

10. Include Everyone
Excluding people often leads to hurt feelings and arguments. Try to make room for everyone who wants to join in the fun.

Real-Life Scenario:
A new student asks to join your game of tag, but someone says, "We already have enough players." You step up and say, "There's always room for one more!" Now the new student feels welcome, and you've prevented a potential disagreement.

11. Learn When to Say Sorry
If you realize you've made a mistake or hurt someone's feelings, don't be afraid to apologize. A simple "I'm sorry" can go a long way in fixing things.

Real-Life Scenario:
You accidentally bump into someone during a game, and they get upset. You quickly say, "Sorry about that! I didn't mean to." They smile and say, "No problem." Problem solved!

12. Know When to Ask for Help
If a disagreement gets out of control or someone is being unkind, it's okay to ask a teacher or playground supervisor for help.

Real-Life Scenario:
Two classmates start yelling during a game of soccer, and it looks like they might fight. You let the teacher know, and they help calm everyone down and reset the game.

13. Celebrate Teamwork
When you solve a disagreement or avoid one altogether, take a moment to feel proud. Handling conflicts is a big step toward being a great teammate and friend.

Real-Life Scenario:
You and your friends couldn't agree on what game to play, but you worked together to come up with a new game that everyone loves. Now you're all laughing and having the best recess ever.

Final Thought
Disagreements on the playground don't have to ruin your fun. By staying calm, listening, and finding creative solutions, you can handle conflicts like a fourth-grade expert. Remember, the goal is to keep recess fun and fair for everyone. So next time there's a disagreement, step up, solve the problem, and get back to playing—you've got this!

Chapter 4 How to Handle Disagreements on the Playground in Fourth Grade

```
V Y O O T I K D G B M U Y U J K X S E E J K K
K X A K A Z A A L B L X G H M Z I B T C M F T
C Z H V R X Q R Y E B W T E A F H E B K A U R
O A O U F Y T W G U D X M I Y A X K T J K L O
R L P E F G I B X H H C F O R F R N E W E G N
B S W F H D U O L X R L F G P U R G Z B R G V
K Z M U C N B O Y X S I S U Y C R W P R O M Q
E A X S W J W K Q P Z Q G W J D R L W E O P I
D F R Y C T U D K M E O T Q Z U D P D A M L H
N E B N F I Y N G P J K P P Y T S X Q T R D V
A V O V C P S E N U D T F L D G C A Y H P H E
T I X C A V E S S Y P O L A R P D U A A S O V
S T N U B H Y J O M D E R Y D D N C P X O E Z
R C N N J R X Q O R Q S G G O X N E T Z L R V
E E S A A V P S H R S I O R G M R G L S U Q P
D P D D A V A S Z M Q M E O E T O I M M T E D
N S A H Z T Q Y P U I O D U T S V P O L I T E
U R M I F P X I B E I R I N Q D J G Y V O P V
R E Y X V C E E W Q P P A D C O U E S U N E F
K P Z W C R P A F P X M K Y V D F J E H S E K
T P E R S O N A L O L O Q V H O S X Z P A D V
G V B I K Z M K O S E C T K D K S P P M V R Y
H Q D A M T T Q L T Y A W A K L A W Y B P Y E
```

breath	personal	scissors
compromise	perspective	share
deep	playground	solutions
makeroom (make room)	polite	understand
paper	rock	walkaway

Chapter 5

How to Ask the Right Questions in Fourth Grade

Hey, future question master! Fourth grade is all about exploring new ideas, solving tricky problems, and digging deeper into what you're learning. Asking the right questions is like having a superpower—it helps you understand more, impress your teacher, and even help your classmates. This chapter is packed with tips, tricks, and real-life scenarios to show you how to ask awesome questions and make your fourth-grade year even better. Let's dive in!

1. Be Curious About Everything
The first step to asking good questions is to be curious. Think about what interests you or what doesn't quite make sense. When you wonder about something, turn that curiosity into a question.

Real-Life Scenario:
Your class is learning about the solar system, and your teacher mentions that Neptune is super cold. You raise your hand and ask, "Why is Neptune colder than other planets?" That one question could lead to a lively discussion about space!

2. Know What You Want to Learn
Great questions have a clear purpose. Think about what you're trying to figure out before you ask. Is it something you didn't understand, or do you want to know more about a specific topic?

Real-Life Scenario:
While working on a math problem, you encounter difficulty with long division. Instead of saying, "I don't get it," you ask, "Can you explain how to figure out the remainder in this problem?" Now your teacher knows exactly how to help you.

3. Ask Open-Ended Questions

Open-ended questions usually start with words like why, how, or what. They can't be answered with a simple "yes" or "no" and help you get more detailed answers.

Real-Life Scenario:
Your class is reading a story about a character who makes a tough choice. Instead of asking, "Do you think they made the right decision?", you should ask, "Why do you think the character made that choice?". Now your classmates can share their opinions, and the discussion gets more exciting.

4. Use Follow-Up Questions

Sometimes, one question leads to another. Don't be afraid to ask follow-up questions to dig deeper into the topic.

Real-Life Scenario:
During a science lesson, you ask, "How do plants make food?" Your teacher explains photosynthesis. Then you ask a follow-up question: "What happens if a plant doesn't get enough sunlight?" Suddenly, you're learning even more!

5. Write Down Questions Ahead of Time

If you know you're going to have a discussion or a test, think of questions ahead of time. Writing them down helps you stay prepared and makes sure you don't forget what you wanted to ask.

Real-Life Scenario:
Before your class reads a chapter on explorers, you write down, "Why did explorers take such big risks?" When the teacher asks for questions, you're ready to go!

6. Don't Be Afraid to Ask

Some kids worry that asking a question might make them look silly. But guess what? There's no such thing as a bad question. Chances are, other students have the same question but are too shy to ask.

Real-Life Scenario:
Your class is learning about fractions, and you don't understand what a numerator is. You raise your hand and ask, "What's the numerator again?" Your teacher smiles and says, "Great question! Let me explain." Suddenly, everyone understands better.

7. Ask Questions That Help the Whole Class

If you're working in a group or having a class discussion, think about questions that can help everyone. This shows you're a team player and care about your classmates' learning too.

Real-Life Scenario:
Your teacher is explaining the rules for a new project, and you notice some kids look confused. You ask, "Can you give an example of what the final project should look like?" The teacher gives a clear example, and now the whole class knows what to do.

8. Use Questions to Solve Problems

Questions aren't just for the classroom, they're also great for solving real-life problems. When something doesn't go as planned, ask questions to figure out what went wrong and how to fix it.

Real-Life Scenario:
You and your group are building a model for a science project, but it keeps falling apart. Instead of getting frustrated, you ask, "What's making it so wobbly? Do we need more support in the middle?" Your group tries your idea, and it works!

9. Learn from Other People's Questions
When your classmates ask questions, listen carefully. You might learn something new or think of another question to ask.

Real-Life Scenario:
During a history lesson, a classmate asks, "Why did pioneers travel in wagons?" You realize you also want to know how they carried food. You ask, "What did pioneers eat on long trips?" Now you're both learning cool facts.

10. Ask About Real-Life Connections
A lot of what you learn in fourth grade connects to the real world. Asking questions about how topics apply to everyday life makes learning more interesting.

Real-Life Scenario:
Your class is studying ecosystems, and you ask, "How do ecosystems affect the food we eat?" Your teacher explains how farms depend on healthy soil, and you realize science is all around you.

11. Turn Mistakes into Questions
If you get something wrong, don't feel bad—turn it into a question! Mistakes are great opportunities to learn.

Real-Life Scenario:
You get a math problem wrong on a quiz. Instead of feeling upset, you ask your teacher, "Can you show me where I made the mistake?" The next time, you get it right!

12. Be Respectful When Asking

It's important to be polite and respectful when asking questions. Wait for the right time, raise your hand, and listen carefully to the answer.

Real-Life Scenario:

You're curious about a topic, but your teacher is in the middle of explaining something else. Instead of interrupting, you write your question down and ask when it's your turn. Your teacher appreciates your patience.

Final Thought

Asking the right questions is one of the best ways to learn, grow, and show off your curiosity. Whether you're in class, working on a project, or solving a problem, remember that good questions lead to great answers. So don't hold back—be bold, be curious, and keep those awesome questions coming. You've got this, fourth grader!

Chapter 5 How to Ask the Right Questions in Fourth Grade

```
B P E D M R X U P Q G X E R B O U P A K T S T
H J B Q E D Z P B I C P U J G R A Q A P V E O
W X D S Q D E X P L O R I N G L Y O G V K J F
X G X K F O N M T R E A L L I F E N H V N C U
H R E W O P R E P U S L Q Y P N B K Z R C H A
D B P S O Z N U V U R O Z W Q X M X J O L B T
Y S Z P Q Y Z C R R E S P E C T F U L A U C
K A A V R J E H H D C F E F B A U A X O S S O
G E A W G D G C K W U T Y T H Q W W J S S V E
V D R P P G T P H B M C F W F A J S U O M W V
J I R H U D S Y R U T P P D G P S I G B A W L
F E F C F E P C V S B M S T C G U P H G T A O
C Q H O T G X C F P F V N X Y N Y L M K E N S
Q K B Y Z K U Z Z Y W P M A W O H E R Z S S C
W O Q M I R X D T Q R E I C U X R H W D H D S
X Z E M I C C Y A W U F B G B Z U U C N N G I
M C M O D H B N U A H E O R E N S F I M L S W
Y M U R A B N A D N Q D S N O V Z A F Q A N C
W S S N S D T H G E I F I T W M J S G Z B G W
F Z W E R C A L F A X D D H I O K G F H Z K U
M X L P P C J T K L I S T E N O S K O Q Y O E
M M E O Q P Y X Y U J L E R V D N Q M T U T N
G V P U P U W O L L O F P W Y Y A S G Z L M B
```

classmates	help	reallife (real life)
curious	ideas	respectful
ended	listen	solve
exploring	open	superpower
followup (follow up)	questions	

Chapter 6

How to Work Together in Small Groups in Fourth Grade

Hey, teamwork champion! Fourth grade is full of cool opportunities to work in small groups, whether you're solving a tricky math problem, building a science project, or creating a skit for class. But working with others isn't always easy. Sometimes people have different ideas, talk over each other, or don't help out. Don't worry! This chapter is packed with tips, tricks, and real-life examples to help you become an awesome team player. Let's dive in and make teamwork a breeze!

1. Start with a Plan
Before diving into your group task, take a few minutes to come up with a plan. Decide what needs to be done, who's doing what, and how much time you have. A good plan keeps everyone focused and on track.

Real-Life Scenario:
Your group is building a volcano for a science project. Instead of everyone rushing to grab supplies, you say, "Let's figure out the steps first. Who wants to mix the baking soda and vinegar, and who wants to paint the volcano?" Now your group is organized and ready to go.

2. Listen Before You Speak
It's exciting to share your ideas, but great teamwork starts with listening to others. Let each person explain their thoughts before jumping in with your own.

Real-Life Scenario:
Your group is brainstorming ideas for a class skit. Instead of shouting out your idea right away, you say, "Let's go around and hear everyone's thoughts first." By the end, you have a mix of creative ideas that make your skit even better.

3. Divide the Work Fairly
Make sure everyone in the group has a job to do. When tasks are divided evenly, the work gets done faster, and no one feels left out.

Real-Life Scenario:
Your group is designing a poster about recycling. You say, "Let's split this up! I can write the title, Sam can draw the pictures, and Mia can color everything in." Everyone feels involved, and the poster turns out great.

4. Respect Different Opinions
In fourth grade, you'll notice that not everyone thinks the same way—and that's a good thing! Different perspectives can make your group work stronger, so be open to new ideas.

Real-Life Scenario:
You want your group to use bold colors for your art project, but someone else suggests soft pastels. Instead of saying, "That won't work," you say, "Let's try both and see which looks best." You end up with the best ideas for a unique masterpiece.

5. Stay Positive, Even When It's Tough
Group work isn't always smooth sailing. If someone makes a mistake or things aren't going as planned, stay positive and focus on finding solutions.

Real-Life Scenario:
Your group is building a tower out of marshmallows and toothpicks, but it keeps collapsing. Instead of getting frustrated, you say, "What if we try a wider base? I think that might help." Your positive attitude keeps everyone motivated.

6. Be Flexible
Sometimes, group plans need to change. Being flexible and willing to adjust makes the project go more smoothly.

Real-Life Scenario:
Your group is creating a timeline for history class, but you realize you don't have enough space for all the dates. Instead of panicking, you suggest, "What if we use smaller writing or fold the paper to make more room?" Problem solved!

7. Speak Up if Something's Not Working
If someone isn't doing their part or if there's a problem, it's okay to speak up—just do it kindly and respectfully.

Real-Life Scenario:
One group member is playing with their pencil instead of helping with the project. You say, "Hey, we could really use your help right now. Can you work on this section?" They refocus and start contributing.

8. Help Each Other Out
If someone in your group is struggling with their part, offer to help. Teamwork is about supporting each other, not just doing your own job.

Real-Life Scenario:
Your friend is stuck on the math part of your group project. You say, "Let's figure this out together." With your help, they understand it better and feel proud of their work.

9. Manage Your Time Wisely
In fourth grade, group projects often have deadlines. Keep an eye on the clock and make sure your group is staying on schedule.

Real-Life Scenario:
Your teacher gives your group 30 minutes to finish a science experiment. You say, "Let's spend 10 minutes setting up, 15 minutes doing the experiment, and 5 minutes cleaning up." Your group finishes just in time!

10. Celebrate Everyone's Contributions
When the project is done, take a moment to recognize everyone's hard work. A simple "Great job, team!" can make everyone feel appreciated.

Real-Life Scenario:
After presenting your skit to the class, you tell your group, "I'm so glad we all worked together. Everyone's ideas made it awesome!" Your group feels proud and ready to work together again.

11. Learn from Challenges
If your group disagrees or something doesn't go as planned, think about what you can do differently next time. Mistakes are just opportunities to improve!

Real-Life Scenario:
During a group presentation, someone forgets their part, and the presentation feels a little rushed. Afterward, you suggest, "Next time, let's practice a few more times before we present." Your group agrees, and the next project goes much better.

12. Have Fun While Working
Group work doesn't have to be all serious. Laugh, enjoy the process, and remember that teamwork is about having fun while getting the job done.

Real-Life Scenario:
Your group is decorating a diorama, and someone accidentally glues a tree upside down. Instead of getting upset, you all laugh and turn it into a "tree falling in a storm." The project ends up being even more creative!

Final Thought
Working in small groups is a big part of fourth grade, and it's a skill that will help you for years to come. By listening, staying positive, and working together, you can turn any project into a success. Remember, teamwork isn't just about finishing the task—it's about learning, growing, and having fun along the way. So the next time you're in a group, put these tips into action and show everyone what an awesome teammate you are. You've got this!

Chapter 6 How to Work Together in Small Groups in Fourth Grade

```
G R O U P S Z V M N X F V R P F E P D D E J O
I U L K B V L Q V X M E C P C W U F G B R Y Y
M M T M M F Q U P L M G E P Q M B V C J V A P
W H Q S I J M K X I G N O Y L T V O Z H U N Y
L Y N A V W B L T S X C Z A W I X U W V P W U
W Z T C E P S E R T K S O B F M U Z Y R D Z W
W H Q G I S G T P E J E X U L J E V H E Q G C
U S E D I A O R N N V N I K E X K X D D V J V
T A U V N C D I Q I P K V Z X I F F F D K K N
U X G A S T K P I N K N E F I P D M T T X A K
J C M I J N E I I G W S E R B Q I H O H L H R
D K L S A Y M T I U Y S M A L L V H K P L F O
B T L S S V K F Q G U S D J E G I Q Y T Q M W
E D D E J U P N Q M J B U I T A D Z T D D W M
S H O Y C N O U O I Z T B H F D E W G Z J X A
U D Y P O I S P C I O K C I Y F N O S O O K E
D B K V I J I R Z R P A O O S P E L Z R G X T
V V A P Q N T C N Y W Q X S U N T R Q U A O M
B F J O E A I I F W O J J Z F Y E S E D O T V
K I G N S G V O P D R G E S W E L H B N R C Q
M E D E K Z E S N P K D P X T E P D S U T P P
Z N S L O X B Y O S P D A X K U D E S U C O F
T K R I I O H C G T T A Z N J R E Y A M T A K
```

different   listening   positive
divide   managetime   respect
flexible   (manage time)   small
focused   opinions   teamwork
groups   plan   work

Chapter 7
How to Crush Fourth Grade History

Hey there, history explorer! Fourth grade history is an exciting journey through the past. You'll learn about amazing events, inspiring people, and how the world we live in today was shaped. But let's be honest: sometimes, remembering all those facts, dates, and names can feel tricky. Don't worry! This chapter is packed with fun tips, smart strategies, and real-life examples to help you rock your history lessons. Let's dig into the past and make history your favorite subject!

1. Treat History Like a Story
History isn't just a bunch of boring facts—it's the story of real people and their incredible adventures. Imagine the events like a movie playing in your head. Who were the heroes? What were the challenges? How did they overcome them?

Real-Life Scenario:
You're studying the American Revolution. Instead of memorizing dates, imagine being a colonist standing up to the British, shouting, "No taxation without representation!" Suddenly, history feels more exciting and easier to remember.

2. Create a Timeline
Timelines are a wonderful way to see how events fit together. Grab some paper or use a big poster board to create a visual timeline. Add important dates, events, and even small drawings to make it fun.

Real-Life Scenario:
Your class is learning about early explorers. You draw a timeline showing when Christopher Columbus, Ferdinand Magellan, and Marco Polo made their journeys. By the end, you see how their adventures connect and remember the dates without even trying.

3. Make Flashcards Your Best Friend
Flashcards are a simple but powerful way to study history. Write the name of a person, event, or term on one side and the key facts on the other. Quiz yourself or a friend!

Real-Life Scenario:
You have a quiz on important inventions in history. You make flashcards with "Printing Press" on one side and "Invented by Johannes Gutenberg in 1440, helped spread books and knowledge" on the back. After a few rounds, you've got it down.

4. Find Connections to Today
History is all around us! Look for connections between what you're learning and your everyday life. This makes the facts stick in your mind.

Real-Life Scenario:
Your class is learning about the Oregon Trail. You realize that your family took a road trip across some of the same states! Thinking about the challenges pioneers faced makes you appreciate how simple it is to travel now.

5. Use Mnemonics to Remember Facts
Mnemonics are memory tricks that help you remember things more easily. Turn tricky facts into rhymes, acronyms, or silly sentences.

Real-Life Scenario:
You need to remember the order of the first 13 colonies. You create a silly sentence like, "New Cats Like Purring Very Much, So They New Jump Down." Each word stands for a colony, like New Hampshire or Virginia. Now you'll never forget!

6. Play History Games
Learning doesn't always have to feel like work. Look for history games, puzzles, or trivia quizzes to make studying fun. Some board games or apps can teach you while you play.

Real-Life Scenario:
Your family plays a trivia game about famous inventors. You learn that Benjamin Franklin invented the lightning rod and used his kite experiment to study electricity. It's a fun night, and you ace the next history lesson.

7. Use Visuals to Learn
Maps, charts, and pictures can help you understand history better. Look at maps of battles, photos of historical sites, or diagrams of how people lived long ago.

Real-Life Scenario:
You're learning about Ancient Egypt and look at a diagram of the pyramids. Seeing how they were built step by step helps you imagine the hard work and teamwork it took to create something so amazing.

8. Tell the Story to Someone Else
One of the best ways to remember history is to teach it. Tell your family or friends what you've learned. Explaining it out loud helps the facts stick.

Real-Life Scenario:
At dinner, you tell your parents about Harriet Tubman and the Underground Railroad. They're impressed with how much you know, and you feel proud (and ready for your quiz!).

9. Ask Questions and Dig Deeper
Don't just memorize facts—get curious! Ask questions about why things happened and how people felt at the time. This makes history more fascinating and easier to understand.

Real-Life Scenario:
Your teacher says, "The Boston Tea Party was a protest against unfair taxes." You raise your hand and ask, "Why was tea so important back then?" Your teacher explains how it was a big part of daily life, and now you get why the protest mattered so much.

10. Act It Out
Get into character and act out historical events. Pretend you're a famous person giving a speech or recreate a dramatic moment with your classmates.

Real-Life Scenario:
Your group acts out the signing of the Declaration of Independence for class. You pretend to be Thomas Jefferson, and saying the words out loud helps you remember what it was all about.

11. Stay Organized
Keep your history notes, worksheets, and handouts in one place. Use color-coded tabs or labels to find topics quickly when you need to review.

Real-Life Scenario:
Your teacher says there's a test on the Civil War next week. You open your history folder, and everything you need is neatly organized. Studying becomes way less stressful!

12. Visit Historical Places or Museums
If you can, visit places related to what you're learning. Seeing history in person makes it more real and memorable.

Real-Life Scenario:
Your family visits a local history museum with a replica of a Native American village. You walk through the exhibits, try tools they used, and imagine what life was like. Back in class, you ace the quiz on Native American history.

13. Use Online Videos and Books
Sometimes, watching a video or reading a fun book about history can explain things in a way that sticks with you.

Real-Life Scenario:
You watch a kid-friendly documentary about the moon landing. Seeing Neil Armstrong take that "giant leap for mankind" makes you feel inspired—and you remember every detail for class.

Final Thought
Fourth grade history is your chance to explore the amazing events and people that shaped our world. By using these tips—like timelines, flashcards, and acting things out—you can turn history into a subject you love. Remember, history isn't just about the past—it's about understanding the present and dreaming about the future. So grab your notebook and start exploring—you've got this, history superstar!

Chapter 7 How to Crush Fourth Grade History

```
Y H C C O Z P R E T E N D Z V J O U H E E M A
F O N N U N X L L U M Q B X C H T Y S I S C I
R Q F H Q W D G D E F S T U U H G G S T I D F
E G O J V C I E A S H C E R A H O H T R F L F
E H M K I S T H E N V I M V K I N F H G W O U
K N G V Y A L T H K I N Z X Z A V C L Z P M Q
H I I C P S I O E X S O I P V B E M U W S S C
U N H L Y Z G D X V U M J A W N X Y R U G G P
X A O S E Y K Z I L A E G M L V G O G V S D R
D X W O B M U O K S L N H O X P C R Z R G X C
L B R A W A I X E X S M I L Z G X R F X L I S
J A E M R P D T S L O X S R P X T E O X S J C
O C P T K F E F D N X X T R K G X J J X F U O
X O E Q M A Z B R N X B O H E X A L W E C H V
E N E N M S I Z A E S R R E D O Z M I R A X C
H N D I N C N L C F W O Y B R L S C E A S M Y
Y E G I X I A T H S T I R A Z D P J J S D D T
R C I K X N G G S Z C V K Y J I O A C K J I O
O T D R R A R W A Y G O M P B U G M B H D L C
T I I T F T O Q L V C D S W R L M B O M F W J
S O T I S I V A F T B W R N B F J O B Q E A W
V N D H S N Z A A E S A E D I P Z X X W I Z I
V S G U W G U E A T V Y Q D B X W B N R K W X
```

connections	games	pretend
digdeeper (dig deeper)	history	story
explain	journey	timeline
fascinating	mnemonics	visit
flashcards	organized	visuals

Chapter 8

How to Succeed in Fourth Grade Math

Hey there, math whiz! Fourth grade math is full of exciting challenges. You'll tackle new concepts like fractions, decimals, long division, and even geometry. It might sound tricky at first, but with the right strategies, you can succeed and even have fun. This chapter is packed with tips, real-life examples, and strategies to help you rock fourth grade math. Let's dive in and make numbers your superpower!

1. Build on What You Already Know

Think of fourth grade math as leveling up your skills. A lot of what you'll learn builds on what you already know, like multiplication, division, and place value. Start by reviewing those basics to feel confident.

Real-Life Scenario:
You're solving a long division problem like 432 ÷ 6. You remember that division is like the opposite of multiplication, so you think, "6 times what equals 43?" Using your times tables helps you figure it out step by step.

2. Use Math Vocabulary

In fourth grade, you'll hear words like denominator, numerator, product, and quotient. Understanding math vocabulary is key to solving problems and following directions.

Real-Life Scenario:
Your teacher says, "Find the product of 7 and 8." You know the product means the answer to a multiplication problem, so you solve: 7 × 8 = 56. **Vocabulary for the win!**

3. Practice Fractions Everywhere

Fractions are a big deal in fourth grade. Instead of just learning about halves or quarters, you'll compare, add, and even multiply fractions. Try using fractions in everyday life to make them less intimidating.

Real-Life Scenario:
You're baking cookies with your family, and the recipe calls for 1/2 cup of sugar and 1/4 cup of butter. You realize 1/2 is bigger than 1/4 because two quarters make a half. Fractions make more sense when you use them in real life!

4. Break Big Problems into Smaller Steps

Some math problems, like multi-step word problems, can seem overwhelming. Breaking them into smaller steps makes them more manageable.

Real-Life Scenario:
The question asks, "If a car drives 300 miles in 5 hours, how many miles does it drive in 1 hour?" First, you divide 300 by 5 to find the answer (60 miles per hour). Focusing on one step at a time allows you to solve it without becoming stuck.

5. Use Visuals and Tools

Sometimes, pictures or tools like number lines, charts, or blocks can make math easier to understand. Don't be afraid to use them!

Real-Life Scenario:
You're learning about decimals, and use a grid to shade 0.75. Understanding the meaning of the decimal and its relationship to fractions becomes clear when you shade three-quarters of the grid.

6. Practice Mental Math

In fourth grade, you'll need to solve problems quickly. Practicing mental math helps you add, subtract, multiply, or divide in your head without needing a calculator.

Real-Life Scenario:
You're at a store and want to figure out the total cost of two items that are $4 each. Instead of writing it down, you think, "4 + 4 = 8." Quick mental math saves the day!

7. Don't Be Afraid to Make Mistakes

Mistakes are part of learning. If you get a problem wrong, don't panic—figure out what went wrong and try again. This helps your brain grow stronger.

Real-Life Scenario:
You calculate 56 ÷ 7 and write 9 instead of 8. Your teacher points out the mistake, and you realize you skipped over 7 × 8 = 56. Now you know to double-check your multiplication facts!

8. Use Real-World Math

Math is everywhere, from shopping to sports. Look for ways to use what you're learning in everyday life—it makes math feel more useful and fun.

Real-Life Scenario:
You're helping plan a birthday party, and you need to figure out how many pizzas to order for 12 people. Each pizza has 8 slices, and everyone will eat 2 slices. You multiply 12 × 2 to find out you need 24 slices, then divide by 8 to figure out you need 3 pizzas. Math saves the day!

9. Check Your Work
Before turning in your assignments, double-check your answers. Look for small mistakes, like forgetting to carry a number or misreading the problem.

Real-Life Scenario:
You solve a subtraction problem, 345 - 128, and get 217. Before moving on, you check your work by adding 217 + 128 to make sure it equals 345. It does, so you know your answer is correct.

10. Ask Questions When You're Stuck
If you're unsure about a concept, don't be afraid to ask your teacher, a parent, or a classmate for help. Questions help you understand better.

Real-Life Scenario:
You're confused about how to multiply fractions. You raise your hand and ask your teacher to explain. They show you step by step, and suddenly it clicks!

11. Turn Math into a Game
Math doesn't have to feel like work. Use apps, puzzles, or games to make practicing fun. Even friendly competitions with friends can make math exciting.

Real-Life Scenario:
You play a card game where each card has a multiplication problem on it. The person who answers fastest keeps the card. By the end of the game, you've practiced your times tables without even realizing it.

12. Keep a Growth Mindset

Instead of saying, "I can't do this," tell yourself, "I can't do this yet." Believing you can improve with practice makes a big difference.

Real-Life Scenario:

You struggle with long division at first but keep practicing a little every day. By the end of the month, you're solving problems with confidence and even helping your classmates.

Final Thought

Fourth grade math might feel challenging at times, but with practice, patience, and the right strategies, you can master it. Remember to stay curious, ask for help when you need it, and celebrate every little success along the way. Whether you're tackling fractions, decimals, or tricky word problems, you've got what it takes to succeed. So grab your pencil, dive into those numbers, and show the world what a math superstar you are!

Chapter 8 How to Succeed in Fourth Grade Math

```
F K T W D H Y P D Z G L M N U B C N W R F E O
C K G E S E P L N Y L M G T P D P T S J Q A T
V T R L J V J B E Q N P C Y R A L U B A C O V
N F H N F K X R B S K Z Z K S G X J M G F N Z
S L O O T J W S T K Y W O U U G C Y C A N X N
S C S K Z U U J P H F L S Q O F K G C Z U S S
H E F O O Z J K C E H C R V A N A N O P H M E
N D Y J N X E J N D T E W I B A G U U F I U I
F K Y B M S R U U Z L S R S S Q X A S J X N G
K E F P A Y U T R L X F W U S J I P X Q G B E
H E M U G Q C T A Z K M O A Q C X S B P E Q T
C Y W Z V L G M N S C D E L F R Q Q B O U H A
R T L Q U E S T I O N S Q S N I V R Q B Y U R
E Z N K U B O R B F D H O S H E P I A H C Y T
T T W Q I L X P R R V L U I E M Z T Z Z F Q S
Q Q I B Q P F I B A N X R F G K E T P M P L A
O H D D A Y F V B C T T B O L J A N L I X M B
B H I R L C F I G T F D B R W O V T T P H W G
C T D C C H X H A I D J W Q X L U Z S A X R G
S A T M A V U R M O O X O V G U A J L I L N X
C M B K J S R G E N I F I V G O Q E M I M L E
C R X S Z V B K M S L E A S U O T F R W U W D
O V Y G Z N V N Z E B P X E C I T C A R P X G
```

check	mistakes	steps
fractions	practice	strategies
game	questions	tools
math	realworld (real world)	visuals
mental	smaller	vocabulary

Chapter 9
How to Read Like A Pro in Fourth Grade

Hey there, fourth-grade bookworm! Reading in fourth grade is a whole new adventure. You'll dive into longer stories, learn big ideas, and tackle tougher texts. But don't worry—this chapter is here to help you sharpen your reading skills, discover amazing books, and understand everything you read. Ready to level up your reading game? Let's go!

1. Find Books That Match Your Reading Level
Fourth-grade books are longer and sometimes more challenging, but that doesn't mean they have to feel overwhelming. Look for books that are just right—not too easy, not too hard.

Real-Life Scenario:
You pick up a book about explorers, but it has so many tricky words that you can't understand the story. Instead, you try a book with shorter chapters and helpful pictures. It's just right, and now you're loving the story.

2. Try Different Genres
Fourth grade is the perfect time to explore different genres like mystery, fantasy, nonfiction, and historical fiction. Trying new types of books can help you discover stories you never knew you'd love.

Real-Life Scenario:
You've always read fantasy books, but your friend recommends a mystery novel. You give it a try and get hooked on solving the clues alongside the characters. Now you're a mystery fan too!

3. Use Context Clues for Tricky Words

If you come across a word you don't know, don't panic! Look at the words and sentences around it to figure out the meaning.

Real-Life Scenario:
You're reading a science book and see the word "habitat." You notice the sentence says, "The desert is a habitat where animals like snakes and lizards live." Now you understand that a habitat is a place where animals live.

4. Take Notes While Reading

In fourth grade, you'll often read to learn. Taking notes or highlighting important parts can help you remember key details.

Real-Life Scenario:
You're reading a biography about Harriet Tubman and write down, "Helped slaves escape on the Underground Railroad." Later, when your teacher asks about her, you remember the important details because of your notes.

5. Visualize What You Read

Good readers create pictures in their minds as they read. Think about how the characters look, what the setting is like, and how the action unfolds.

Real-Life Scenario:
You're reading a book about a shipwreck, and you imagine the waves crashing and the sailors scrambling on the deck. Visualizing makes the story come alive, and you feel like you're right there.

6. Ask Questions as You Go
Great readers are curious. Ask yourself questions while you read to keep your brain active. What's going to happen next? Why did the character do that? How does this connect to what I've read before?

Real-Life Scenario:
You're reading a story about a boy lost in the woods. You wonder, "Will he find his way out? What tools will he use to survive?" These questions keep you hooked until the end.

7. Summarize What You've Read
After finishing a chapter or a section, try summarizing it in your own words. This helps you remember what happened and makes sure you understood the main ideas.

Real-Life Scenario:
You finish reading about the water cycle and tell your classmate, "Water evaporates, turns into clouds, and then falls as rain or snow. That's how it works!" Explaining it out loud helps you remember it even better.

8. Read Aloud for Expression
Reading out loud isn't just for younger kids. It helps you improve your fluency and understand how sentences flow. Try using different voices for characters to make it even more fun.

Real-Life Scenario:
You're reading a play for class, and try giving each character a unique voice. Everyone laughs at your "angry pirate" impression, and you feel proud of how well you brought the story to life.

9. Set Reading Goals
Setting goals can make reading more exciting. You might aim to finish a book in a week or read 20 minutes every day.

Real-Life Scenario:
You challenge yourself to finish a new graphic novel over the weekend. By Sunday night, you're turning the last page and feeling proud of your accomplishment.

10. Look for Themes
Fourth-grade books often have themes or big ideas, like friendship, bravery, or teamwork. Pay attention to what the story is trying to teach you.

Real-Life Scenario:
You're reading a story about a girl who helps her neighbors after a hurricane. You realize the theme is kindness and community, and it makes you think about how you can help others in real life.

11. Don't Skip Nonfiction
Nonfiction isn't just about facts—it's full of amazing true stories about real people, places, and events. Use nonfiction books to explore topics you're curious about.

Real-Life Scenario:
You love animals, so you check out a nonfiction book about wildlife conservation. You learn about endangered species and even get ideas for your next school project.

12. Discuss Books with Friends
Talking about books with friends can help you understand them better and make reading more fun. Share your favorite parts, characters, or what you think might happen next.

Real-Life Scenario:
You and your friend are both reading the same mystery book. You say, "I think the butler did it!" Your friend disagrees, and you laugh as you debate the clues together.

13. Use Technology to Boost Reading
There are lots of apps and websites that make reading more interactive. Some let you listen to audiobooks, while others have fun quizzes about books.

Real-Life Scenario:
You download an app that reads a story aloud while you follow along. It helps you understand tricky words, and you finish the book feeling like a reading rockstar.

14. Stay Curious
If something in a book sparks your interest, dig deeper! Look it up online, check out more books on the topic, or ask your teacher for recommendations.

Real-Life Scenario:
You read a book about ancient Egypt and get curious about mummies. You check out another book about pyramids and even watch a documentary at home. Your curiosity turns into a mini-history adventure!

Final Thought

Reading in the fourth grade is all about exploring new ideas, diving into longer stories, and challenging yourself to learn more. Whether you're flipping through a mystery novel, exploring a nonfiction book, or solving puzzles in a story, remember that every page is a chance to grow. So grab your next book, turn the page, and start your next reading adventure. You've got this, fourth grader!

Chapter 9 How to Read Like a Pro in Fourth Grade

```
N M D D O M G X K T N H Z K P V Z J M B K N Z
D C H U F S I I W M D R L Y M A H Q M N O B E
G W L R C M S B E I M P E G E N R E S B U Z X
B Z F U A I G R D D Y F Y A L G M P O V I N T
E V T F E S P E C N C G J S D P X C G R L R O
G Z Y Q H S D Y B H P E B M X A C L A A F Y A
R K K P I G K I Z G E Q N Y S H L M M C J J Q
U Q S Y S Q Y H Q O S M Q N S X M O K T Y W H
V V T H Q C F D U A F R M Y G U G U U Y I C Y
K M L V S E T O N L O N G W S A C L K D R O P
I C S I F L A I T S A O O L I I Q T T V H I D
D C E V E B V Q H H L F D N P L A Y R Y Z R N
N Y R V Y N I Z K O E N F Y F D B N G S H B D
U Q E O L Q C B N X W M X S B I J Y Y R M O E
P L J E K J Q H J O J Y E N K B C M C E J Z R
G O F W P E C P R D Q D X S C N E T F N I O S
S C C W U E F D T C X J E H G O C S I L M A P
R K X K T F S Q X X Q K C D G P Z B A O P C D
Y R O C P U L J E Q B D D O P I Z U P G N B F
C A C O R B P N T K M S N O I T S E U Q S E Z
J I S S B N W A N R U A S V K I H L F A Y Z J
Q Y S J Z G X L O Q R T B K V S S W Q D Q S D
R L S H C U E F C J J U U T G U C Y H Y G M K
```

books	level	summarize
clues	nonfiction	technology
context	notes	themes
genres	questions	visualize
goals	readaloud (read aloud)	words

Chapter 10
How to Succeed in Fourth Grade P.E.

Hey there, future athlete! Fourth-grade physical education (P.E.) is not just about running laps or playing games—it's about learning how to work as a team, staying active, and developing new skills that can help you on and off the field. Whether you're already a sports superstar or just looking to have fun, this chapter is full of tips, tricks, and real-life ideas to help you rock fourth-grade P.E. Let's lace up those sneakers and get moving!

1. Set Personal Goals
P.E. is a great time to challenge yourself. Maybe you want to run faster, improve your basketball shot, or finally climb that rope in the gym. Setting small, achievable goals will help you improve step by step.

Real-Life Scenario:
During your P.E. fitness test, you realize you can only do 5 push-ups. You set a goal to reach 10 by the end of the semester. Every week, you practice a little more, and when the next test comes around, you crush your goal!

2. Be Open to Trying New Activities
Fourth grade is all about exploring new skills. You might try a sport or activity you've never done before, like volleyball or yoga. Even if it feels unfamiliar, give it a shot—you might discover something you love.

Real-Life Scenario:
Your class is learning how to juggle scarves, and at first, it seems silly. But after a few tries, you start to get the hang of it. By the end of the lesson, you're having fun and showing off your new skill.

3. Focus on Teamwork
In fourth-grade P.E., you'll play a lot of team sports. It's important to support your teammates, share the ball, and cheer each other on. A good team player helps everyone succeed.

Real-Life Scenario:
You're playing soccer, and a teammate misses a shot. Instead of getting upset, you say, "Great try—let's get it next time!" Your positive attitude keeps the team's energy up, and you all work harder together.

4. Pay Attention to Instructions
Your P.E. teacher gives directions to help everyone stay safe and understand the rules of the game. Listen closely so you know what to do and avoid getting hurt.

Real-Life Scenario:
Your teacher explains how to do the hurdles safely, but some classmates aren't paying attention. You focus and learn to lift your knees just right. When it's your turn, you soar over the hurdles like a pro while others struggle.

5. Practice Sportsmanship
Winning is fun, but being a good sport matters more. Shake hands after games, congratulate others, and stay positive—even if you lose.

Real-Life Scenario:
Your team loses a close basketball game, and you feel disappointed. Instead of pouting, you say, "Good game!" to the other team. Later, a teammate tells you how proud they are of your great attitude.

6. Stay Active, Even Outside of P.E.

The skills you practice in P.E. get even better when you stay active outside of class. Play sports, ride your bike, or join an after-school team to keep moving.

Real-Life Scenario:
You join a weekend soccer league and notice that your passing skills improve during recess games. By the time you're back in P.E., you're one of the best players on the field.

7. Dress for Success

Wearing the right clothes and shoes helps you perform your best and stay comfortable during P.E. Make sure you have sneakers and clothes that let you move easily.

Real-Life Scenario:
It's your first day of P.E., and you forget to bring sneakers. Running laps in boots is no fun, and you feel slower than usual. After that, you always check your bag the night before to make sure you're ready.

8. Warm Up and Cool Down

Your teacher will lead you in stretches and warm-up exercises to get your body ready for action. Cooling down afterward helps your muscles recover.

Real-Life Scenario:
Your class warms up with jumping jacks and stretches before running laps. At first, you think it's boring, but later, you realize your legs don't feel as tired. Warming up makes a big difference!

9. Learn to Problem-Solve

Sometimes, disagreements happen during games—like who's out in dodgeball or whose turn it is to bat. Practice solving problems calmly and fairly.

Real-Life Scenario:
Two classmates argue about whether a ball was in or out during volleyball. You suggest, "Let's replay the point so it's fair." The game continues smoothly, and everyone appreciates your quick thinking.

10. Celebrate Small Wins

Improvement doesn't happen overnight. Celebrate the little victories, like running one extra lap or hitting the target in archery for the first time.

Real-Life Scenario:
You've been working on your underhand volleyball serve, and after weeks of trying, the ball finally goes over the net. Your teammates cheer, and you feel like a champion!

11. Stay Hydrated and Energized

P.E. can make you sweat, so don't forget to drink water and eat healthy snacks to keep your energy up.

Real-Life Scenario:
After a long game of kickball, you grab your water bottle and take a big gulp. You feel refreshed and ready to tackle the next activity without getting tired.

12. Be Patient With Yourself
Not every skill will come easily, and that's okay. Keep practicing, and remember that everyone improves at their own pace.

Real-Life Scenario:
You struggle with dribbling in basketball and feel frustrated when your classmates seem to get it right away. Instead of giving up, you practice during recess. A week later, you dribble down the court like a pro.

13. Have Fun and Stay Positive
P.E. isn't just about exercise—it's about having fun, making friends, and enjoying the process. Keep a positive attitude, and don't forget to laugh and enjoy yourself.

Real-Life Scenario:
Your class plays a silly game where you hop like frogs to pass the finish line. Even though you're not the fastest, you laugh so hard that it becomes your favorite part of the day.

Final Thought
Fourth-grade P.E. is your chance to move, learn new skills, and have a blast with your classmates. Whether you're playing a team sport, practicing a new activity, or working on your fitness, remember that effort and a positive attitude are what truly matter. So get out there, give it your all, and have fun—you're going to crush it this year!

Chapter 10 How to Succeed in Fourth Grade P.E.

```
E X A V V C N A B U E X G L I E D H L X D T H
X T G D L Z X A T C P V G V F Z Q M O J N W N
H W L U C O K A C T I V E C G U D U I I F K O
M G N I V L O S C M Z O N M N I S S H N W W O
L K W E G I J C D Y F F L N K R T C K F U J B
H B P E E G N G U I F K H U Y S N R B R N F L
H P K I U I L S Z W O K R Y E P E Y E G E H X
U B N M H R L M T X V Q Y S D V I G Q O W X P
P V V R X S Z H P R N G D B U R T G M A T X Y
W K N V L K N W V J U H L N C M A L Y L H H X
B W A F B E Y A A I I C F B A K P T S S I V V
M Z J L U O X K M Z A V T G T O P H E D N C Z
L H C G T C J L I S K K Q I I Z L R O D G J E
R T T M P S L B Y B T T C D O J N M Q P S T V
L L H D Q H K C I J M R T E N N M U J W A Z L
M R A M U A S V J P L E O T Y J S Z A R B H C
B N T C V X M A L X A G H P B F Q R B X H E F
Z Y S Y I W U R K M R F D T S V C E R F Y L Q
F S X J G S I B W U W K V K D N L D W I X R J
P U M R A W Y O O I V A M P C E O S M Z H I D
I E P A H W R H W D Y J I F C G G U C M V Z J
G Q T C X K A O P B N M G N W O D L O O C U A
A R L Q B Z A L C U Y K V I H F I B S T E R B
```

active	goals	physical
celebrate	hydrated	solving
cooldown	instructions	sportsmanship
education	newthings (new things)	teamwork
fun	patient	warmup

Chapter 11
How to Rock Fourth Grade Science

Hey there, science superstar! Fourth grade science is all about exploring, experimenting, and understanding the world around you. From electricity to ecosystems, you'll learn about amazing things that make the world tick. But science isn't just about memorizing facts—it's about asking questions, making discoveries, and having fun. This chapter is full of tips, real-life examples, and strategies to help you succeed in fourth-grade science. Let's get started and uncover the secrets of the universe!

1. Stay Curious and Ask Questions
Science is all about curiosity. If you wonder how things work or why something happens, you're already thinking like a scientist. Don't be afraid to ask questions during class—they can lead to fascinating discoveries.

Real-Life Scenario:
Your teacher is talking about volcanoes, and you wonder, "Why don't all mountains erupt like volcanoes?" You raise your hand and ask. Your teacher explains the difference between volcanic and non-volcanic mountains, and suddenly, you feel like a geology expert.

2. Get Hands-On During Experiments
In fourth grade, you'll do more experiments than ever. These are your chance to see science in action! Pay close attention to the steps, follow the instructions carefully, and take notes on what happens.

Real-Life Scenario:
Your class is testing which materials conduct electricity. You connect a paperclip, a rubber band, and a pencil to a circuit. When the light bulb turns on with the paperclip, you learn it's a conductor. Hands-on learning makes it easier to understand.

3. Use a Science Journal
Scientists always write things down. Keep a science journal to record observations, draw diagrams, and jot down ideas. It helps you organize your thoughts and remember important details.

Real-Life Scenario:
Your teacher asks you to observe the phases of the moon for a week. You draw pictures in your journal each night, showing how the moon changes. When it's time to share your findings, your journal helps you explain it clearly.

4. Learn to Love Charts and Graphs
In fourth grade, you'll use charts, graphs, and tables to show data. These tools help you make sense of your experiments and explain what you've discovered.

Real-Life Scenario:
Your group is measuring how far a toy car rolls on different surfaces. You record the distances in a chart, then create a bar graph to compare the results. The graph makes it easy to see that smooth floors are the fastest!

5. Connect Science to Real Life
Science isn't just something you do in school—it's everywhere! Look for ways to connect what you're learning to the world around you.

Real-Life Scenario:
Your class is learning about ecosystems, and you think about the pond near your house. You notice frogs, birds, and plants all living together. Suddenly, ecosystems aren't just a lesson—they're part of your everyday life.

6. Team Up with Classmates
Science projects often involve teamwork. Working with your classmates means sharing ideas, solving problems together, and learning from each other.

Real-Life Scenario:
Your group is building a model of the water cycle. One teammate suggests using cotton balls for clouds, another cuts out a sun, and you create the raindrops. By working together, you make an awesome model that impresses the whole class.

7. Use Technology to Explore
There are so many cool apps, videos, and websites that make science fun and interactive. Use them to dig deeper into topics you're curious about.

Real-Life Scenario:
You're studying planets and find an app that lets you zoom in on Mars. You explore its craters and mountains, and it feels like you're an astronaut on a space mission!

8. Practice Explaining What You Learn
Being able to explain what you've learned is an important skill in science. Use your own words to describe a concept, and don't be afraid to use drawings or models to help.

Real-Life Scenario:
After learning about the water cycle, you explain it to your younger sibling using a glass of water and a hairdryer. You show how water evaporates, turns into clouds, and falls as rain. Your sibling is amazed, and you feel like a science teacher!

9. Pay Attention to Patterns
Science is full of patterns, like the phases of the moon, the growth of plants, or the behavior of animals. Recognizing patterns can help you make predictions and understand the bigger picture.

Real-Life Scenario:
You're observing how seeds grow in sunlight versus shade. You notice that plants in the sunlight grow taller and greener. Recognizing this pattern helps you understand how plants need light to survive.

10. Read Science Books and Articles
Sometimes, you'll find answers to your questions by reading. Look for kid-friendly books, magazines, or websites about science topics that interest you.

Real-Life Scenario:
You're curious about black holes, so you check out a book from the library. It explains how black holes form and why nothing can escape their gravity. Now, when your teacher mentions them, you feel like an expert.

11. Don't Be Afraid to Make Mistakes
In science, mistakes are just part of the process. If your experiment doesn't work the way you expected, it's a chance to learn and try again.

Real-Life Scenario:
You're building a bridge out of straws, but it keeps collapsing. Instead of giving up, you try a new design and use tape for extra support. On your third try, the bridge holds up a stack of books, and you feel like an engineer!

12. Have Fun With Science
Above all, enjoy the process of discovering new things. Science is about exploring, experimenting, and being amazed by the world around you.

Real-Life Scenario:
Your teacher asks you to create a "mystery box" experiment where classmates guess what's inside based on clues. You fill your box with objects and watch as your friends use their science skills to solve the mystery. Everyone has fun while learning!

Final Thought
Fourth-grade science is your chance to explore the wonders of the world—from the tiniest cells to the vastness of space. By staying curious, working hard, and having fun, you'll uncover amazing things and become a science superstar. So grab your lab coat, start asking questions, and get ready to make discoveries. You've got this!

Chapter 11 How to Rock Fourth Grade Science

```
B K C I K E W B O S M S T Y R P A T T E R N S
G I A I K Z D Y T C T Q O L J O U R N A L E H
X A B T T U B S Z J J C H Z W A S C E Q H P G
Z J A T L W P U K P C A E I C I J G G T V G B
R T X A N H B B B I X Z T J Y A C M G D B T Y
W G X E E T U T E C H N O L O G Y M E Y Z F B
V S I O X L H G B K Q V U G R R I V I W A L Y
A F C L P A G X C J U C I A W S P W Z J T S O
N G M G E E Y S U G T J P M T G D Z C R Y P B
X R H K R B N H K S X H R A K M D R E J S D E
J G W X I C N O A G S J K I T G Z T F E F A N
E Y W H M X M K I A G E P V I C P Q J C V P E
K F R E E J S B N T S E T V J P P O G U Z Y X
Y Q P Q N W S C I S C D X D V N M M C K N D P
S L Y Q T D R Y C N H E D J R N L L K Z X S L
U H E S S Y K G R L K I N N R S I C U J E N O
O W M Z T Q Y Y H J Z I C N G E G A E J L O R
I L T I C U M E M T L Q T L O Q Q I L L B I E
R A Q K H E I G Z K E C N E I C S N H P E T E
U N P C A Y M P N G U B A U N D R R H K X S D
C R V T R H S U K V C V A V G Y M I G C F E A
B U H I T U G T P J Y Z T Z B K L B F V U U S
N B G W S H S O W J J Q Z C X W C E Z N N Q K
```

charts	explore	patterns
connection	fun	projects
curious	graphs	questions
experiments	journal	science
explain	mistakes	technology

Chapter 12

How to Write Like a Pro in Fourth Grade

Hey, fourth-grade author! Writing in fourth grade is all about turning your ideas into amazing stories, essays, and projects. It's not just about getting the words on the page—it's about organizing your thoughts, adding detail, and making your writing shine. Whether you're writing a story about a pirate adventure or explaining why recess is important, this chapter will help you take your writing to the next level. Let's get started and make your words work for you!

1. Start with a Strong Plan
Good writing begins with a solid plan. Take a few minutes to organize your thoughts before you start. Use a graphic organizer, outline, or brainstorm your ideas.

Real-Life Scenario:
You're asked to write about your dream vacation. Instead of jumping in, you make a quick list:

- **Where:** Hawaii
- **What to do:** Surfing, hiking, eating tropical fruit
- **Why:** It's sunny and exciting!

Now, when you start writing, you know exactly what to say.

2. Hook Your Reader
Your first sentence is like a fishing hook—it needs to grab your reader's attention! Start with a surprising fact, a question, or an exciting description.

Real-Life Scenario:
Instead of starting your essay with, "Dogs are great pets," try: "Imagine having a best friend who's always excited to see you, no matter what. That's what it's like to have a dog!" Now your reader is hooked.

3. Use Vivid Details
Details bring your writing to life. Describe how things look, sound, smell, taste, or feel so your readers can imagine it perfectly.

Real-Life Scenario:
You're writing a story about a camping trip. Instead of saying, "The forest was nice," write, "The forest was alive with the rustling of leaves, the chirping of crickets, and the smell of pine trees after the rain." Now your readers feel like they're right there with you.

4. Organize Your Ideas
In fourth grade, your writing needs to have a clear beginning, middle, and end. Use paragraphs to separate your ideas and keep everything in order.

Real-Life Scenario:
You're writing about why you love pizza.

- **Beginning:** Introduce your topic and grab attention: "Pizza is the best food in the world, and here's why!"
- **Middle:** Explain your reasons, like the delicious toppings and gooey cheese.
- **End:** Wrap it up: "Whether it's pepperoni or plain cheese, pizza makes everyone smile."

Your writing flows smoothly, and your readers stay interested.

5. Add Dialogue to Stories
Dialogue (what characters say) makes stories more interesting. Use it to show how characters feel or to move the story forward.

Real-Life Scenario:
In your story, instead of saying, "Max was scared," write:
"'Did you hear that noise?' Max whispered, his voice shaking. 'It sounded like a ghost!'"
Now your readers can feel Max's fear and excitement.

6. Use Transition Words
Transition words help connect your ideas and guide your reader through your writing. Words like next, then, because, and finally make your writing smoother.

Real-Life Scenario:
You're writing about how to build a treehouse. Instead of listing steps randomly, you use transitions:
"**First,** choose a sturdy tree. **Next,** gather your materials. **Then,** build the floor and walls. **Finally,** add a ladder so you can climb up."
Now your readers can follow along easily.

7. Revise Like a Pro
Great writing doesn't happen in one draft. After you finish, go back and revise. Look for places to add details, fix mistakes, or make sentences clearer.

Real-Life Scenario:
You write: "The dog ran fast." After revising, you change it to: "The big golden retriever sprinted across the park, chasing the red frisbee with all his might."
Your sentence is now vivid and exciting!

8. Check Your Grammar and Spelling
Before you turn in your work, check for mistakes. Look for missing capital letters, incorrect punctuation, and spelling errors. Use a dictionary or ask a friend if you're unsure.

Real-Life Scenario:
You accidentally write: "their going to the park." During editing, you realize it should be: "They're going to the park." Fixing small errors makes a big difference.

9. Practice Persuasive Writing
In fourth grade, you'll often write to persuade. This means convincing your readers to agree with your opinion. Use strong reasons and examples to make your argument.

Real-Life Scenario:
You write an essay about why your school should have more recess. Instead of just saying, "Recess is fun," you write:
"Recess helps us stay active, which is good for our health. It also gives us a break so we can focus better in class. More recess means happier, healthier students!"
Now your argument is strong and convincing.

10. Experiment with Different Types of Writing
Fourth grade is the perfect time to try different styles. Write stories, poems, how-to guides, or reports. Each type of writing helps you learn new skills.

Real-Life Scenario:
Your teacher asks you to write a poem about the seasons. You've never written a poem before, but you give it a try:
"Winter whispers through the trees,
Snowflakes dancing on the breeze."
You discover that poetry is a fun way to play with words.

11. Read to Improve Your Writing
Good writers are also good readers. Pay attention to how authors describe things, build characters, or create suspense. Use what you learn in your own writing.

Real-Life Scenario:
You're reading a mystery book and notice how the author drops clues to keep you guessing. In your next story, you hide a clue in the first chapter, and your classmates are amazed when they realize you were hinting at the ending all along.

12. Celebrate Your Progress
Every time you write, you're getting better. Celebrate the little wins, like finishing a story, improving your handwriting, or using a new word.

Real-Life Scenario:
You struggle with writing long paragraphs but finally complete a full-page story. Your teacher says, "Great job using details!" You feel proud and excited to keep writing.

Final Thought
Writing in fourth grade is your chance to share your ideas, tell incredible stories, and make your voice heard. By planning, revising, and adding vivid details, you'll create work that makes your readers say, "Wow!" So grab your pencil, let your imagination run wild, and write your heart out—you've got this!

Chapter 12 How to Write Like a Pro in Fourth Grade

```
X Y E C I E X W E S Q T V T N E O J G G T N V
Q L N V A E I A K H S V D D P H C M T A B X F
I V Q D S F S L D Y N B A D Q H E O H K H J S
W X M I J B G I I M F S E D F G P W M X O E Y
L G C A Z G U T V R C D R H G K Y Q K M T O F
E A Y L V U F J U E G N I T I R W Y E A J G H
V O C O K L I R J M R G A C C E S E R Q U Q Y
Y P Y G R P K Q T E P U I F Z T K B U R P K B
X G R U Q L Q G M R W X C I B Q E R T P W B K
G S G E S G H Q W E E S N N Q L B R F R R F E
J N Q T X I A P C H J A I O E J R V Q D U W N
J A H P B F O D Y W G W T C L S F Q E Q X V O
R S N R T Z A G X R R F B K G H E T A K M A I
Y O Q P W R A Y O Z C F A N V G A I M B M X T
T M B S V C F R P Q N J I Y Y I O L I P B B I
R K N H S U J R L F A L G W L O P R R E U L S
T X G W G W B S K G L C N S E G U H Y H Z L N
C I C R I E G W V E Z O G U Y Q H H J Z I N A
Q M T E Q V F L P S O I E W L R A M M A R G R
N J F X B Q K S J H M P Z A B B W U R H G C T
E R F K T S M O S W L L Z X K Y W X S N A L P
Q R K V P B D P X I D T X X Y G H M Z C Z K R
S F E U V Z R J O Q U W T B O S Y N D O B E O
```

celebrate   organize   transition
details   plan   what
dialogue   read   where
grammar   revise   why
hook   spelling   writing

Chapter 13

How to Conquer Fourth Grade Homework Like a Pro

Hey, fourth-grade homework hero! Homework in fourth grade can feel like a big step up. There's more of it, and sometimes it's harder, but guess what? You can handle it! With a few smart strategies and some practice, you'll be cruising through your assignments like a pro. This chapter is full of ideas, real-life examples, and tips to help you stay on top of your homework, keep your stress low, and maybe even have a little fun along the way. Let's dive in!

1. Create a Homework Routine
The first step to conquering homework is to have a routine. Choose a specific time and place to work every day. When you make homework part of your daily schedule, it feels less stressful.

Real-Life Scenario:
You decide to start homework every day at 4:00 PM, right after your snack. You sit at the kitchen table because it's quiet and has good lighting. After a week, it becomes a habit, and you don't even think about it anymore—it's just part of your day.

2. Keep a Homework Planner
Fourth grade means more subjects, which means more assignments. A homework planner is a lifesaver! Write down your assignments every day, including due dates, so nothing gets forgotten.

Real-Life Scenario:
You have a science project due next week and a math worksheet due tomorrow. You jot both down in your planner. When you open it after school, you know exactly what to tackle first—no surprises!

3. Break Big Projects into Small Steps
Sometimes, homework feels overwhelming, especially when it's a big project. Breaking it into smaller steps makes it more manageable.

Real-Life Scenario:
You need to write a report about an animal for science class. Instead of trying to do it all at once, you break it into steps:

- Day 1: Pick your animal and find facts.
- Day 2: Write the introduction.
- Day 3: Add details about habitat and diet.
- Day 4: Edit and finish.

By spreading it out, the project doesn't feel like a huge mountain to climb.

4. Start with the Hardest Task
When you sit down to do homework, tackle the hardest subject first. Your brain is freshest when you start, and getting the tough stuff out of the way makes the rest feel easier.

Real-Life Scenario:
You have a tricky math assignment and an easy reading worksheet. You decide to start with math. Once you finish, the reading feels like a breeze, and you're done before you know it.

5. Eliminate Distractions
Homework time is focus time. Put away your phone, turn off the TV, and find a quiet spot. The fewer distractions, the faster you'll finish.

Real-Life Scenario:
You usually do homework with music on, but you realize it's slowing you down. You turn it off and finish your assignments 15 minutes faster. Now you have extra time to play!

6. Use Homework Helpers
If you're stuck, don't be afraid to use tools to help. Websites, apps, or even your textbooks can explain things in a new way. Just make sure to double-check your work.

Real-Life Scenario:
You're confused about how to simplify fractions. You watch a short video about it online, and suddenly it makes sense. You finish your math homework with confidence.

7. If You Need Help, Ask
If you don't understand something, ask for help! Your teacher, parents, or even a classmate can explain things and get you unstuck.

Real-Life Scenario:
You're struggling with your spelling words. Your mom quizzes you, and your older sibling shares a trick for remembering the tough ones. By test day, you're ready to ace it.

8. Take Short Breaks
If you have a lot of homework, take a 5-minute break every 20-30 minutes. Stand up, stretch, or grab a quick snack to refuel your brain.

Real-Life Scenario:
You're working on a long social studies worksheet and start feeling tired. You take a short break to stretch and drink water. When you come back, you feel refreshed and ready to finish strong.

9. Check Your Work
Before you pack up your homework, take a few minutes to check for mistakes. Look for missing answers, spelling errors, or anything that doesn't make sense.

Real-Life Scenario:
You finish your math worksheet but notice you wrote "18" instead of "8" in one problem. Fixing it before handing it in saves you from losing points.

10. Reward Yourself
Motivate yourself with a small reward after finishing your homework. It could be extra playtime, watching your favorite show, or enjoying a snack.

Real-Life Scenario:
You tell yourself, "If I finish all my homework before dinner, I can play video games for 20 minutes." The reward keeps you focused, and you finish in record time.

11. Stay Positive
Some days, homework feels hard, and that's okay. Remind yourself that every assignment helps you learn and grow. Keep a positive attitude, and don't give up.

Real-Life Scenario:
You're working on a tough writing assignment and feel frustrated. Instead of quitting, you take a deep breath and think, "I'll just do my best." By the time you finish, you feel proud of your effort.

12. Pack Your Bag the Night Before
Don't let all your hard work go to waste by forgetting your homework at home. Pack your backpack the night before so you're ready for school.

Real-Life Scenario:
You double-check your bag before bed and realize you almost forgot your history worksheet. Crisis averted! The next day, you turn it in on time.

13. Learn From Mistakes
If you make a mistake, don't stress! Use it as a chance to learn and do better next time.

Real-Life Scenario:
You get a math problem wrong because you skipped a step. Your teacher shows you how to fix it, and now you know how to solve similar problems in the future.

Final Thought
Homework doesn't have to feel like a chore. With a good routine, focus, and the right attitude, you can tackle any assignment that comes your way. Remember, homework is a chance to practice what you've learned and show how much you're growing. So grab your pencil, get started, and show that homework who's boss—Let's go!

Chapter 13 How to Conquer Fourth Grade Homework Like a Pro

```
C Q M L J E J S K E I I N A K V M M T X P V E
Q F P Y X M V M Q C Y H S A W B R O V U H T B
P U P S D Z U U H B V M L P S R Q Y C M A A C
C W E K Z P S F P S X I K X K U E V H N J L E
J M F S P P E V Z X R C D R A W E R I H V K Y
I G G A T V L W L Z C F K N E Z I M R E B J S
E E Y I Z I K I G C H D U D R D I B E L I N K
T C E S S D O J Z N O I I B B L T J T P C O T
M S I S I B P N N M P B Y N E A G E K E F L Z
A S D T Q Y V X S R P Z X G B S P Y D R E X I
N O Z E C Z M U L L A D D P S O M U S S W U
A W J U N A O Q A A D H I X K O S A Z Q N L K
G M I R N A R N G P B Q S S Y P I N W N E P V
E T N O A Q N P S U N D T E X P T D Y U R B K
A U P K U E Q Z B E O Y R K O N I C A X F L V
B K I X R P X I X V Q I A A E E V F U C B I I
L M C V D O W G L F D W C T G N E D L T K B Z
E P F E P D W N I N R U T S H I U K Q S S X Z
F Y S T H W F E R V F G I I K T J Q C K T W A
B S X S R C N M M S E B O M O U A Q I N I W M
S A D S Z O Z D L O X H N D L O W F E T R Z Z
Y Z Y M S L F A Z K H F S Y J R F Y J Y N R C
K Z D N U F M D S B S Q K M M Y O C Y V Z I K
```

breaks	homework	practice
check	manageable	questions
distractions	mistakes	reward
eliminate	planner	routine
helpers	positive	turnin (turn in)

Chapter 14

How to Ace Fourth Grade Exams

Hey, fourth-grade superstar! Exams might seem like a big deal, but with the right strategies, they don't have to be scary. Think of studying for exams as training for a big game or preparing for a performance—you practice, get better, and then show what you've got. This chapter is packed with ideas, real-life examples, and tips to help you prepare, stay calm, and do your best on exam day. Let's get started and show those exams who's boss!

1. Know What to Study

Before you dive in, make sure you know exactly what's going to be on the exam. Ask your teacher for a study guide or review your notes to see which topics are most important.

Real-Life Scenario:
Your teacher says the math test will cover fractions, multiplication, and word problems. You write those topics at the top of your notebook and start reviewing them one by one, so you're focused on the right material.

2. Make a Study Schedule

Don't wait until the night before to start studying! Spread your studying out over several days, focusing on a different subject or topic each day.

Real-Life Scenario:
Your science exam is in a week. On Monday, you study the water cycle. On Tuesday, you focus on ecosystems. By Friday, you've covered everything and still have time for a quick review. No cramming necessary!

3. Create a Study Space
Find a quiet, comfortable spot where you can focus. Keep your supplies—like pencils, highlighters, and paper—close by so you don't waste time looking for them.

Real-Life Scenario:
You clear off your desk and turn off your tablet so there's nothing to distract you. With your notebook, a glass of water, and your favorite pen, you're ready to study like a pro.

4. Use Flashcards
- Flashcards are a fun and easy way to practice facts and vocabulary.
- Supplies Needed: Index cards (any size of your choice)
- Write a question or term on one side of an index card and the answer on the flip side.
- After creating the flashcard, read the question and then the answer.
- Read both sides of the card without trying to memorize the answer.
- Repeat the above step over and over
- Do this repeatedly each day. Soon you'll realize that you know the information without really trying to memorize it.
- Test yourself or ask a friend or family member to quiz you.
- **This works!**

Real-Life Scenario:
You're studying for a history test and making flashcards for important events. One card says, "What year did the Declaration of Independence get signed?" You flip it over: "1776." After practicing a few times, you've got it memorized.

5. Try Study Games
Turn studying into a game to make it more fun. You can create quizzes, make a matching game, or even set up a "Jeopardy!"-style challenge with your family or friends.

Real-Life Scenario:
You and a friend are studying spelling words. You play a game where you get a point for every word spelled correctly. The person with the most points at the end wins a small prize (like a piece of candy). It makes studying way more exciting!

6. Use Diagrams and Drawings
Sometimes, drawing pictures or diagrams can help you understand tricky concepts. This is especially useful for science and math.

Real-Life Scenario:
You're studying for a science test and draw the water cycle with labels like evaporation, condensation, and precipitation. Seeing it on paper helps you remember how it works.

7. Summarize in Your Own Words
After reviewing a topic, explain it in your own words. This helps you figure out if you really understand it.

Real-Life Scenario:
You're studying ecosystems and write, "Plants are producers because they make their own food using sunlight." By putting it in your own words, you make sure you truly get the idea.

8. Practice with Old Assignments
Go through old homework, quizzes, or worksheets. These often have similar types of questions to what you'll see on the exam.

Real-Life Scenario:
Your teacher gives back your math quizzes from earlier in the semester. You practice solving the problems you got wrong the first time. When similar questions show up on the test, you're ready.

9. Ask for Help
If there's something you don't understand, don't hesitate to ask a teacher, parent, or friend. Sometimes, hearing an explanation in a different way makes all the difference.

Real-Life Scenario:
You're stuck on a long division problem, so you ask your teacher for help during recess. Your teacher shows you a new method, and suddenly it all clicks. Now you can solve those problems with confidence.

10. Take Short Breaks
Studying for hours without a break can make your brain tired. Work for 25-30 minutes, then take a 5-minute break to stretch, grab a snack, or rest.

Real-Life Scenario:
You're reviewing spelling words and start to feel tired. You take a quick break to do 10 jumping jacks. When you sit back down, you feel refreshed and ready to keep going.

11. Practice Test-Taking Skills
Sometimes, studying isn't just about knowing the material—it's about knowing how to handle the test. Practice reading questions carefully, underlining key words, and checking your work.

Real-Life Scenario:
You practice a sample reading test and underline words like main idea and author's purpose. When you take the real test, those strategies help you focus and answer correctly.

12. Stay Positive
It's normal to feel nervous before an exam, but don't let it overwhelm you. Remind yourself of all the hard work you've done and believe in yourself.

Real-Life Scenario:
The night before your math test, you start to feel anxious. You take a few deep breaths and say, "I've practiced this. I'm ready." The next day, you walk into the classroom feeling calm and confident.

13. Sleep and Eat Well
Your brain needs rest and fuel to do its best. Get a good night's sleep before the exam and eat a healthy breakfast in the morning.

Real-Life Scenario:
Instead of staying up late, you go to bed early the night before your science test. In the morning, you eat eggs and toast. You feel energized and ready to ace the test!

14. Review One Last Time
On the day of the exam, take a few minutes to review key points. This helps you feel prepared and keeps important facts fresh in your mind.

Real-Life Scenario:
You arrive at school early and flip through your notes about the American Revolution. When the test starts, you feel confident because the information is fresh in your brain.

Final Thought

Studying for exams doesn't have to be stressful. With a good plan, some fun strategies, and a positive attitude, you can tackle any test like a champ. Remember, exams are just a chance to show what you've learned—and you've got this! So grab your notes, start practicing, and get ready to crush those fourth-grade exams. Good luck, superstar!

Chapter 14 How to Ace Fourth Grade Exams

```
S S V L B C E W L M Z G Z O K R Q W L Y K U J
F G V F P W S J W V Y W R T J L Y D U T S M C
X H N O Z M B B L L U H W K V H G K F D S D V
B J F I A M S N I V T M I L D J V J Q C J C Z
R N Y X W S R I Y L J L N L X S T J T Q G A Z
S Q E X U A U N N W Z G L N U I E M S Z P F C
N O L S C V R C A L F W A R N J K J Q X L M B
C V N N O N E D Q W I G A M H E H X B A M H D
B N I O V X G F Y M G V R K E R W T S W B Y J
V J W I Q R A I M P P R C I W S S H R C A Q U
N G A T K X N U A O O C R M V B C U P D V Y E
O Y F S E E X I Z M S L J Q O A V D Z V L I C
H S O E J C T X Z Q I S M A R G A I D A J O I
D M C U D M C F K B T W J D B V U K B V Y H T
S W G Q T E C A P S I S S G G Q K L H O G Z C
U I A N U J V W Q Y V Y X L H S E P W O U G A
M B V Y U D T N O V E V U V L N E V K U N I R
M G B R Z K G I R H S R B W R E B W T I A S P
A Q M Q A A V F O N A S R C L M X I K Y E B Q
R R G G P P R P A F Y U E S S Z F C K L Q I J
I O O V I B R W M G J K A S C H E D U L E F U
Z T K U N K A A Q L V A K W Y H L F J R M X G
E K I Z Z E F I G H O K S Z C H R V U U T I F
```

breaks	flashcards	schedule
checking	games	sleep
diagrams	positive	space
drawings	practice	study
exams	questions	summarize

Word Search Solutions

Chapter 1 The Big Day: Conquering the First Day of Third Grades

```
V F R S O R M F S E I L P P U S W H X H J V J
L J T E J N A P X W I Q Z M I P Y V K Q R W
I L V C S B V Y C U R I O U S M M I B L F H B
M E P U B Q O L F U D E R Y A C B U L K V G
G S G U B T T N D E K J S F M P R A C F A
S Q V M M Z U C R P N K H O O Y X M E U D A C
J S V U Y Z Y X W B H E U L W Z R A C G R D Y
A B S A F N S C W R V P I K I E C P Z H U P O
W L M Z D N F Q O P F X A R K C R L F J S O E
K T S I Q U Y N W J G K M A F Q Y P K U N K C
P G F R S D H A D O W L E A U T Z T U Q N S Q
T H X E I D R L C T I R Z C K P L R L P A M L
H P L I K U O F G I B T E V U E H R C H R I R
I U I T H G V I R E J F G E N I T U O R P L H
R K Q F N B K G C O I N D S Z M G T J Y X E B
D P L A D J L I W R G E N L U N C H T I M E V
G G G T W Y Z B S Q C N Q K O A A Q I P C G R
R S Z T R G I T P X R W E U V F K Y L D L T V
A U U B E C D N I R H Q G H C Q F X G M A V T
D A A Q B A M W O H N F B R W A F B O W K U J
E G J U Y L O M F W P W H Q X L F O N U V O S
G T E I Z U F Y P I E O X U T X U T Z U O M R
D D P V I A C O N Q U E R D E N V P T D X Q F
```

121

Chapter 2 How to Pick the Right Friends in Third Grade

```
G R D I G B A C Q L P S Y X D Y F H A E S V L
G Z Y T I L A U Q Y R D L D T F I N Z B J J Z
Z A O U P X T L G N G R M T W D F U U B I M G
Z Y K M E T S L U D R B V W U Z W F V C T Y E
R X R O P C E T I F D R B B R N O M L L H F M
R N L V W U N Q E B T Y M H D Q T M Y R X E C
H D N E I F O Y X F A H E B L L G Q X P Z H O
S F J O P T H Y B W A P G O Z K G Q Y R P Y N
T D X N P K I N D N E S S U L E U O H N I A A
R I N E U C V A H A X X L Q O H V M J Q H B H
D X S E T D Y S A J V N L R A H Q X E L S D A
N W H E I N X X K E T O Z T R T E U C D B M
V P U C G R L B O B N Y Z I P Z Q W V M N N C
F T H K R B F C J P X J G Y P M B L A H E X V
M Y N M D G T W F I Q I U W Q N T Y H V I O J
X R F L D B V B E L E P P D D W C Y K U R X V
C I G F U G X U S X B B M W P D O Q M G E C J
F G Z L H I R A O M E F U N H N L H X X O L C
F H L U W H M Z G O C V D B D H P F W M J R J
J T R B O P Y F T E E L B A T R O E M O C M Z
W C C Z S Q C Q M F N E T S I L Y O V P A U C
I Y C O K E S Q K K Y U C C I R N B H Q O C Y
V Y F F H H C K I V V T F L Y B F P U O M R R
```

Chapter 3 How to Handle Disagreements in the Third Grade Classroom

```
I D J N R V V R Y O H I D B C F B T G K S I Z
T N H E E J I U U C S D I N Q W N H Q P X N G
J K L N W Y N E O T C W F B E J C R R U B X F
Z A L F E B S M A W A D S O E V A W F D Q O M
X Z U L N O P T D I S A G R E E M E N T G R Z
V O E E V R E E P G J U J U W G G L S H W F G
M P P P O M D D S B J T N R J Q C H V P H H W
M U W M E Z I P B L X E G R F L L D Y D J Z T
S E N F I F H N E Y Y V M R A Q F U R H M Z
D S T F O R G I V E N E S S H E N T Z O U I C
E S P U T D R U H X W K E Z Q T S N L L Q C L
Z E M O T I O N M T W X H M Y K Q P L G R Y U
U V K Y A H W G V W P C Y M L U Q W E N Q L F
B R Q R O O C I N R G X B E W A J Z Y C L H M
D O T P W B O G E H I L G L M G C R P A T E M
J M G Q B M P S H M U L S B I O N Y C W K L C
F Q G T J Y S O H U P Q J O C O O H A P V P P
D M B Z A S C Z V Q I C Q R X C I E D T C J
E Y U H J O D Z I A C F E P Z T N W Y M S G N
Q S X B X T I F F D P T C F J E I O I Y S R P
Q O M U V V F I U R P A C E E W P O P J A R T
M H L W Q L B V P L S N H B O C O X O E D E J
T W W I O Y Z W S Y Y E M U J T L M L J K A J
```

123

Chapter 4 How to Handle Disagreements on the Playground

```
W N D U K P G D M A E W Z H M Z P R O U M P R
K N W N H A H Q M U D T U L M M P Y G Y K K K
K B F D R P H P Y A W A K L A W N W L U Q R G
J D D E O E O G Q V N N I N A Y G Z G V N Y B
U C B R S R W I C H R V B V D V H O L J N J Y
D M S S I V U C L A O D L O M G H L L Q J A K
U C F T V Z B P W M Z K U L H H Z R T M T I C
S B X A R Y E T F R B I F K Q C I E Q M L K O
V R Y N E C L G Z Y S I E V I T C E P S R E P
A A E D P H M W U N I S M L V H J L Q O C Q B
Y J Y C U X A Q R G Q R P H B W A Y G H P V X
S B P X S A K U T L K I F Q L Y U Y I P W P Z
G B K K J V T H Q M F D V Y G G X I L V Q A P
Q Z Q E E G F X H W Q W D R S L M P R L S Y F
B V I O N A Y G S T O G O A Q A X B O G C J T
U B P I L E S P E D H U B Q P N J I C Q I B N
T X K O T H I Q U V N N X D P O D L K Z S T F
X A Q R A I G R G D Y N X R F M L L T C S O G
T A G R J B I A B R Y T O R T A S O I Z O U Q
D O I W R E S F L J T B L V Q B V J G N R K J
I N J V L Y U Q M E L R Y G H N H R H I S E C
G M T C Y H Z V U E Y S Q I J Z Q L E O Z D Q
I S U B O I H T M P Q M W M K E S O L V E E J
```

Chapter 5 Asking the Right Questions in Third Grade

```
K O L P I C Z G Q I X G H M M H V Y C A T G F
S Q O E A M K U O V M P N Z U C Y D B X Y Q J
A L A N J M N V J F U E M I Z O C R T H L A L
N Z Q V I L C P X R M C Y Y R U L J N L K F V
S Z I V G O U P K C A N V W O T E Z X Z Z B D
N Y J Z D E D Q N I S D Q S U D K W S K W I Z
P S P E C I F I C Y C F A T D G E K N B E R A
C K B G J P Q C T P L A R K Y P J S O X Q O E
Z D N I P N M T I M I N G G X Z V G I W N P C
T S I V Y R V A G A X G E C Y O X K T Q I W Q
W M V Q R L V F D E S C Z U V Z A V S I A I E
B B W K Q S O T W M H N W X D G T A E M L Z C
P O M K O J T L H R H G O Q R V P O U P P G U
H X H G Q S T H E L M W X C U E O D Q O X H R
F M G O B M L E R K N X Z Y X Q I R V R E P I
O S H T S Z B F E H W T H N X H T Q F T L F O
N K H X J N S P W X A W B L P O I E L A L G U
H K N T K N P Q J H K V P T M S V E O N W K S
S D T Y F P D O W P P S R O T V A N L T N O F
B C A M O E V G Q Q X H F N M R C Q Y C A A I
G F Y P H M L S W S M R A F N T C Y M T M H J
N T B S W G B Z N B W I Y E J T X W V P L W C
X J K U K W S J Y X M S C M S I L W W Q S S H
```

Chapter 6 How to Be a Great Team Player in Small Groups

```
C R X O Z B J O H S T B S M A L L S S U X J P
I E Q C Z C E B R H S O U K O U C O D U F O C
Y G G G X U M R P A I N G N K K F D K X E W G
A T T K B B K P S R V D Y E T Q G B P L K L N
L R A E R W J H P I A S J Z T S T F G M D V I
T E A M W O R K L N N U E N S H P G M J F M N
U O Q Q E J Y D A G K I Y G B E E U E O P E
K V L H K M H U Y J W V B M A P E R O E D B T
R U A I M H E V E N N W L B J R R P U R K V S
F L R C H G L O R Q B N W S S D U Q M F G N I
Q Y P S N M T L W E P F Z Y G I A O V F K M L
B Z J S B Q K E T E P B J X X Z E U C Z D D N
S A E D I F C A R N K O F K L W Y F C N I M M
B R Q Z X B M Y N M Q K J U S U N N C O E A T
I P T C X M E R G E Q D E H X F S U N G E C D
Z O D Q A B D M D J P K W H N A L N Z T X W V
Y P L E V V H R W C C R P S X E G F G H L G P
G R T J J O D N E P B S S Z O T X Y V Z M R W
H G F Q W P V M Y M X S K S P G N O I N I P O
S D H C F I T S A U O A E S I D X W Z N C X H
K A Q X L C I O L F X T J P D R Q O J S Z D P
Z F Q L D H I G E A D F O C F L R Q C J C X J
J Z J H T G E Y Q N Z H D B V W C O W G S K D
```

Chapter 7 How to Succeed in Studying Third Grade History

```
Q F H S U W R S E W R I T E G C H E X D J U H
C K Z C O V X U V W C S L S H A S Q P R T V A
W D Q L K N V Z S Q T W D X C U Z R F J X O U
F J P W E K V U T J Z L G X N H K T Z H D N S
Q X M Q X K I K N S T N B Y S V H P O U C U A
M O X M Q O K B M S K Z U Z F U Q X Q N W F N
L K J H I S T O R Y Y H A L T V O Q Y N H M G
I L G Z K E Q Z C S D X Y R Y U V I T W V T G
K E C H F I U W I O U L B O Z I X B R B F E X
P Z M A G V Q R E N T R A P Z Q U R W U B X M
A Q F Y T X J I G M S O T F X A W J F I C X E
K A G I Q U E S T I O N S R T G T E Y Y O P Q
Z T H Y Z A V E M M X I Q V X R W Q G R H X C
X Z P D Y E V N N J R R W X B S V N D S H W L
N D M N Y R O T S I P F V W T S L A U S I V U
C G C L F F Y V O K L Z E U N G S G A X I Z Q
C V M R E A L L I F E D J K N X R S N X Z R
Z L D X I H U G N B H Y M O L M S I E G Q F I
V U E U D R D H O W I A R I O J C M M D W A K
H X T M J Y H C V N G M W O T S D F A E A C L
C U Z T K I E T G E U G N N Q B B U G A Y T K
H P V N N C Q P W V W S M W F T I R S V Q S J
I B Q R L Q C H G P L K S Z A M F Z X Z Z N B
```

127

Chapter 8 How to Succeed in Studying Third Grade Math

```
H B T A V D Y H J E R D U K H H A D I U F B G
T G K P R A C T I C E M N O F Z G M L E G N B
V L L Z M G F K E R N K S W Z B P Z X O I Z X
O V A I F U M E U E I O W P R M A Q J V D C O
G Z D H P X Y Z F B G S Z D E R M J L I E Z G
Q D O S S X I G O M G H V G W T Y O Z M D K D
S Q E U S M L A I E W H C Y X B S J P S W R B
B B P T I L R Z O M K I A L H P R L Q H V V M
I L E J E W P P Q E L U O X T D S G O T E Z E
Q C T F V C N W E R W B I U L E P L D Y Y X W
K I Z N Y S T U N P N M F S Z C B L H Z D F C
M Q R J U X I I X L O L J Z F W S A N X T T X
I S Z N Y S Y R V B A R F X N X W M S S Q Z L
M A T H V R K B R E L L S A I Q V S P K K T P
E C J U X B F N A Y Q U E S T I O N S J H K O
L L J K C D F F M K C C F L Y T P S P V Q L C
O F Z P J T U M G G D A K Y S T T T Z O P X S
I O K Z M L R S K C I R T S D O R Z M G S W D
Y N B O U B X O R T S P T Y S D S K A A E D O
A I K D V P K N H F L P Q M W N O R C P O X E
S S X X U F F T S P L T S Y H X T I E L C F
C X M M V Q I O E N W I S G L C J F R H H Q N
T O A H Y T G S Z M K W L K L A B Q H G A C Z
```

Chapter 9 How to Become a Reading Rockstar in Third Grade

```
K B B U U L L C X B Y Y J U K L T Q F H T M I
N O T Y N Z E D E Y N O B Z H Q E R S W M M A
O I H S Z U J D B R P S B S T R A T E G I E S
J O X O O M F S E R I P Y O X Z X D U O L A Y
P U Q T V O V T A P M Y O Z Z C R D W S N X R
V O C X F V H C E M S J I O Z U Q K E O J N
Q U X A Q R T S Y I R R N C G B T K D G V
O W N U O I A W R J D A V G S U N S H L B Z J
Q Z O T C U G E S O R E I R L W I E K O F F P
G U N E V N G B R M R K M P A L D I G S D A I
M J F L Q Q N F A S N L U V O O A M U I U N E
P O I Z O G S D A W Y B A E G V E R C V I E H
A B C P K Q G T K G F G B Y A X R I N B Z O T
M C T K K V I P D H J G N O I T A N I G A M I
X Q I W M O E V E R Y D A Y Z F N D Z K T Q A
N L O J N P D M F D Q A U W L H L X O D K E T
G I N P K M X R U Q I H E C A U U H I C M O L
N F T B I U J S B O Z G T O F K U S F F F Z
C A W Z D U A B B X H S C O T T K M A W T D T
E X J R L O T U T O J W T B P O H H P V Z Y Q
V V R B R S M G P Z W A J O O S E G H D X C U
J J C C Q D B J G Z T N Z B D S E L N S H X Y
G H O Z G U E A Y Q K L G C E X O R X H R F W
```

Chapter 10 How to Crush It in Third Grade P.E.

```
X S C I V G H I X O M B A C D T G I K K Y C O
X U F F H P D W R N G L M Q V V Z E M P E E Y
F D H N W W F N P Q P I Y D Y X M H H F E Z Z
B W N Z Q Z M A V V B Y R M D W C Y D B K A Q
Y B T C A X S M O R Z U S V V M S A O G F C M
C R I I Z B K F D K A E Y G V I T T G S C E W
Q O A M W G W N J K E Z T S C F Z Q B B U D S
X H X I W C O C O M Y E M A P R N G U V F M O
Q W V U O R E L P I S D L Z L M S O H W N F U
L K W V J R O Z G P T D U A R R O G M A A R F
B Q B E H U Q F O V F A U W R T E L A T A S M
T I E L F X S K I N C M C R R M L I S E G K N
R W O Z V P F W D Y F B U O D N E G M B F E
I E K Y P R R K J G M L H V D V I L A L B L C
R A Y X I U Z P V K E K J M A E T S V R V A I
J K E A S U V H A S R T S T I A F D D S N V T
P Q H B L B R L T T P W G E L T W E R S T N C
C J Q I Y P I V Q B W W C Z I A T L R W R S A
E C A V E S M Y B T N H H L R A A Y S R O R R
I N I L T G H Q M O Y K H M R K H T X F F R P
E U O E Z W A H T F F Y U D X I I Y R W F O W
O G N R U R S J D U S P Y S K A S S J B E L S
P J G T U W J T B N B H R N D N N H U C P Z B
```

Chapter 11 How to Be a Science Superstar in Third Grade

```
F M K D Y T D W W D T K X J T Y W C B P I W T
V H Y Q O V O R F W F T S F V N R S R P P J S
M W A H H Z E T S E Y S K B T C Y C L I R E R
Y P M V A K J G U O A N D F Z X N I I O L O O
R I V F W U J A U W U O M I N C U R V G P L A
V N Y C U D Z Q A Z R I K S D J O G G Y H T L
G U Q F T J P J V A C T C P Z G O O Q P V N S
N H W U W X X D Q F E S W W B L G X S R E P I
R A T S R E P U S T D E E D O X W F Q R Q U K
V E Q V E I Z V J E M U J N H M D R N S Y C A
Z C U R I O S I T Y N O H P L J R F F Q R W R
E X P E R I M E N T S C N U P F G C L K K P M
A W B C I Z S R S A E F G C B W H A N D S O N
F C C B I M P T O I G A E K Z G Q V U D F B M
S M H O H L O X O Q O R I S K R T X O R E W S
U P J U Q L V W B N P J O T L K Z J D T A W E
S M W P A M V W L H W H U W X V C E Y T P W P
E L V A J D H A Y T N G Z S T V X R C D M P A
N N I S W G N L F P R C R J A F R H W W S R S
S X C V B R K R D O Q J R B W S W D P X X X T
E T G V U I Z B U C G I D Y C Y R S B L C Z N
S N O O Z Y Q P L V H F C G F P E C N E I C S
L I J M V I T D X B N S V T B Q C C D P A Q T
```

Chapter 12 How to Rock Third Grade Writing

```
R D R T G P X A W W S D G V O R T R C J O T I
I O I M A G I N A T I O N G S L G T O P Z B L
S K A P A S C D C Z R R F U S V O N E T S S W
G A F N P D K K N U U A X M P Q B Z I K C C L
Z C K D Z R W X G E A V N M X W T Q Q V S X I
C U V G R O C X P N L Z Y S R N Q Y C A O V A
I G G I U W N P C I L I I S I M M L J E K Q
A X U F S E N T E N C E S C F T B G M C F D S
C P K P K U K Z U P P Q N K W Y I J G I M P I
J Q B N I T Y P V K Z C G Z T B F O W X O Q D
W N G D R R A L Y N X S S N Z I I B N P D V J
U N Y S B Q P Z E R A H S U I H W D U O M Y F
F I H D I Z I Q T R C L O H H T D G T I D E R
K C A B D E E F Q B Q A P J L R I X Y B V O G
P H M A E I W H A S X C O S X A R E I I V K
I L X V T P E R S U A S I V E J F P W L Z W M
N Q C V A U K Z P Q V R Q U Q H E L E A M J M
U Q S E I E O H X E V O M U H Q P O G R V P S
M C P L L R I D A F E J M Q Q E D J T G T R Q
F Y W R S G N W W X I F N L P R A C T I C E P
Y N K S A T W A Z L A I Q F Z O X Q L T A C T
A S G B H W C D J Z W B K P V A E B C H F J B
K X J N Z X N X D T E S J G A B T U J N J T Q
```

Chapter 13 How to Conquer Third Grade Homework

```
U F R E O F C Q W W W E U B B B D P W W B D I
C K R O O B C A Z R T U P R E W A R D X U M O
P Q A T C H Y Z N A E Y D A E F A O E G Q E Z
E U N T V A C I N D Z E Y I L K W D E R F I N
D T A S S O V I B D F N K I B N A K D C Z S W
Y A E M Q J M T R H I N R G A I L M Q W X V U
L T U U E L U P V M F Z Z N Y A Z G H P J U M
C S L X I R H A S W J A Q C O V Q A O H H S C
O U W E N O Z X S Y W Y G W J N J N R A V X O
P D S I S K K S B T F J R S N D J S F C W O H
Q U N V P P Y W O I N Z F K E X E U R N L J L
G Y X I U Y X I R W M U A S A D J Q C J Z R K
Y V R C B N D S B Q P W K B I Y Q S B E G W F
T W H V R C O V B Q X Y K S B T D Q I C V M D
H G O X E L O X D F L E T C S F L O Z A Y H Y
Z K Q I A Z I K X F D R Y G U A C S U L N H M
E Y D X K B P L K J A A J F Y H H N B P C E R
E S K U S F T C Y C P L E H O F O B C O Q A O
K S G C Z A B V T L Q Z H O L S L M D S D M A
C L G W E F G I H O M E W O R K Z P U O I G Q
A O Y V Z H O W H W M Y S E L U D E H C S C J
H S C Q I N C F I X V H N O R G A N I Z E J F
K O K Y S F C O U W K Z G R O E R U Z L E W I
```

Chapter 14 How to Be an Exam-Ready Rockstar in Third Grade

```
P R S X D S W O S J K T M X B K G I C B N S R
K I X Y J Y C C P A X O U E A U A B F J N R M
A Z V Y B E Y Y Z Z H P C Y M Q K S J O L C A
E A C I E Q O P O R C S X N R O Q W I W N F S
K G Z A J T P S E F W T K E S W R T J K L C D
L E O E G D B N I P Q B Z Z P C S Y O A B X B
V H N J K B T G R F S Z B P V E V I S A U X K
X W P F A R X A Z M U K X C U S B H C R R J P
Q J W E A Q C P Q Z B K A Q T N C D Y G P G A
E Q E P O T U H A Z L D S E R A K W F G G C N
C G L N I H F Z G R Q L H Z R L Q V S Q P S L
J V D C C G E P E N B U K D N B Y L H Y R F X
R S E L K O R L H H A G S Z P Y E G V M Y B R
M A X E J R Z A G W D H F T D E Z M S Q V J E
X P H V Y V S N G T D H P H P Q K F Q E N E A
U W A I G P K J W V G V R W S G C W N H T J I
E W E T B V E M E M J S U E S T N A W V U O S
Z J Z O R B F K W Q Z E G K G W U H E X K G N
M Z E T N W Z P G P F A Q N H Q T D E T Q X B
P U Q F B Y K N Q S S U A E C B U H Y K X N T
L X C S M L X G R W Z P L E A T Y X W F R M Z
K G F R G J V A M P G V O U I M Q K O S Z V Z
Y K T B K J I Y L P T T O Y K N Q I Z I I N V
```

Other Books by Bobbie Anderson Jr.

- Third Grade Survival Guide
- Fifth Grade Survival Guide
- Sixth Grade Survival Guide

www.ingramcontent.com/pod-product-compliance
Lightning Source LLC
Chambersburg PA
CBHW051950290426
44110CB00015B/2189